ST ANDREWS

ANCIENT CITY IN THE TWENTIETH CENTURY

Betty Willsher

Published by

Librario Publishing Ltd

ISBN: 1-904440-24-X

Copies can be ordered via the Internet
www.librario.com

or from:

Brough House, Milton Brodie, Kinloss
Moray IV36 2UA
Tel /Fax No 00 44 (0)1343 850 617

Cover Photograph: The Scores Walk
(Photo by Andrew G. Cowie, courtesy St Andrews University Library)

Printed and bound by Antony Rowe Ltd, Eastbourne

ST ANDREWS

Ancient City in the Twentieth Century

Betty Willsher

2002

Librario

Previous publications by the Author

School Before Five	1959	Faber and Faber Ltd
Tales of Professor Popoff	1961	Pergamon Press
The Flying Jacket	1964	Blackie and Son
Call Me Person	1969	Pergamon Press
Stones (with Doreen Hunter)	1978	Canongate
Understanding Scottish Gravestones	1985	W & R Chambers & CSA (reprinted Canongate Books)
How to Record Scottish Graveyards	1985	CSA
Scottish Epitaphs	1996	Canongate Books

CONTENTS

ILLUSTRATIONS

ACKNOWLEDGEMENTS

I would like to thank the following for their help: Beatrice Copson, Isabel Dominiak, John Frew, Gordon Christie, Susan Keracher, Terry Lee, John Lindsey, Julia Melvin, Lyn Moir, Julia Prescott, Ronnie Rusack, S.B. Taylor, Penelope Uprichard and the staff at the University of St Andrews Library.

I am also grateful to Alistair Reid for permission to publish his poem, *Scotland*; The University of St Andrews to quote from Mabel Irvine's book *The Avenue of Years*; Jim Crumley and Alan Taylor to quote from articles; Gordon Christie for Map of St Andrews.

And with gratitude to my daughter Penny Walker.

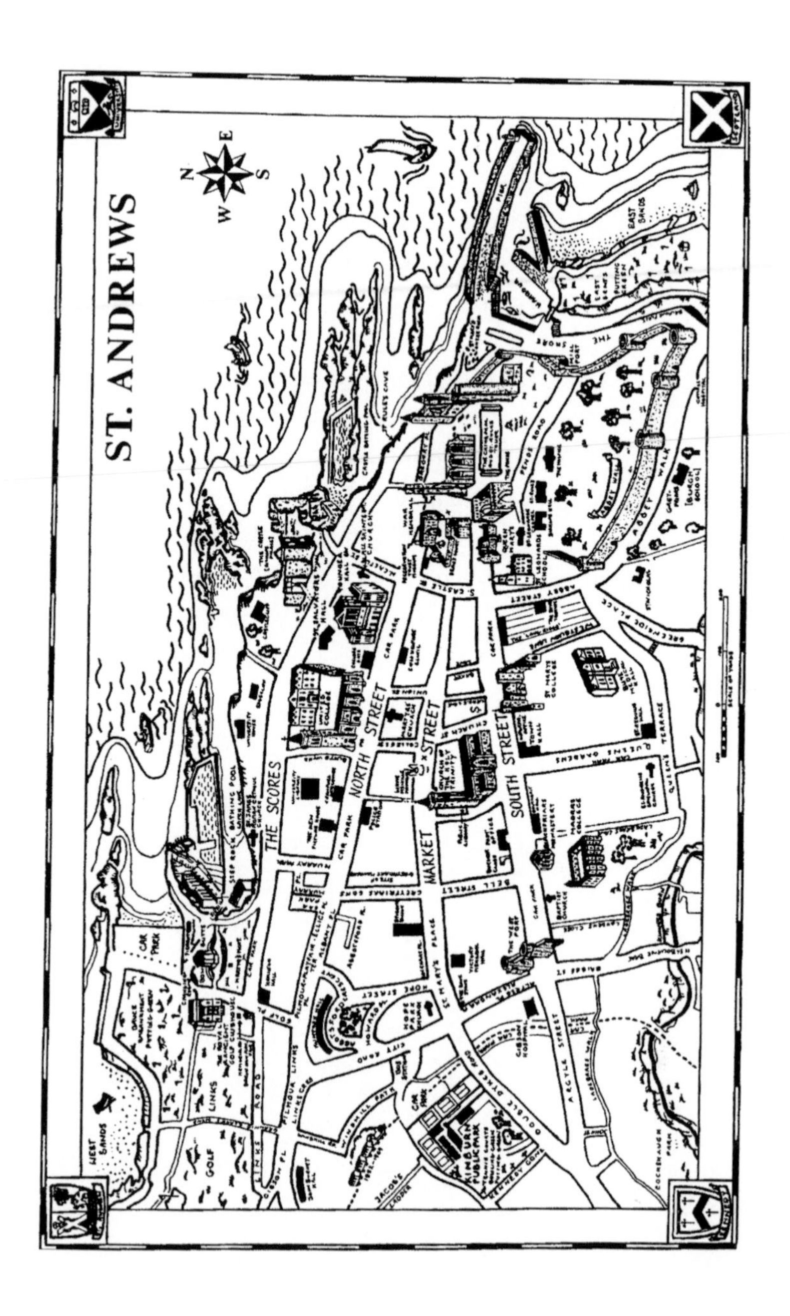
ST. ANDREWS
N
E
S
W
WEST SANDS
EAST SANDS
GOLF
LINKS
CAR PARK
THE SCORES
NORTH STREET
MARKET STREET
SOUTH STREET
STEP ROCK BATHING POOL
CASTLE BATHING POOL
ST RULES CAVE
THE CASTLE
PIER
HARBOUR
THE SHORE
PENDS ROAD
ABBEY WALK
ABBEY STREET
GREENSIDE PLACE
QUEENS GARDENS
QUEENS TERRACE
BELL STREET
GREYFRIARS GDNS
HOPE STREET
ST MARY'S PLACE
CITY ROAD
ARGYLE STREET
DOUBLE DYKES ROAD
PILMOUR LINKS
LINKS CRES
GIBSON PL
GOLF PL
KINBURN PUBLIC PARK
JACOB'S LADDER
THE WEST PORT
MADRAS COLLEGE
ST LEONARDS SCHOOL
UNITED COLLEGE
CHURCH ST
S. CASTLE ST

Chapter 1

INTRODUCTION – A SENSE OF HISTORY

Having lived in St Andrews for fifty-four years, I decided to write about some of the changes which took place here in the twentieth century. Many of the changes were common to other Scottish burghs. But each has its unique setting and its special history.

The past of St Andrews is recorded in thousands of books, documents, papers and legends. The reminders of its story are frequent and forceful. To get the feel of St Andrews you must abandon your car and walk, walk everywhere, sense the contours with feet and eyes. Stride along the three broad main streets which run from west to east on the elevated ridge of rock and converge on the walls and towers of the Cathedral precinct. Stand high on Kirkhill above the harbour and pier. Stroll westward along The Scores, peaceful spacious and dignified, on the edge of cliffs and sea and city. The road slopes down to another revered green precinct, the Links, where six golf courses are laid out for the pleasure, frustration and companionship of residents and visitors. The flag flies proud on the Royal and Ancient Clubhouse. Another more recent flag along the stretch of yellow sands indicates the triumph of a 'clean beach status'.

City Brae will take you up on to the ridge again. The real gateway to the city is the West Port at the west end of South Street. But leave it on your left and go down the hill to find our small river, the Kinness Burn, once vital for its mills, and follow it to the East Sands. The familiar landmarks seem to change position. As you move they gyrate. The relationship between the high towers of Holy Trinity and St Salvator's do not stay constant. Nor does that between St Rule's tower and the Cathedral gables. In the dentist's waiting-room I studied an aerial photograph of St Andrews: a bird's-eye view of an area girdled by the North Sea and heavily packed with solid stone buildings, the wide main streets clearly visible. One late autumn afternoon, after walking home to my cottage in Greenside Place, I wrote the following poem.

Displaced Moon

The man who sweeps the corner of our town
garners the rounded heaps of withered leaves.
He only smiles in Spring, in Autumn's dour
when each day's work is overnight undone.
The sun hangs low and fiercely blinds my eyes,
dark silhouettes of people come and go.
A gold serrated leaf spread-eagled sticks
on moist grey path mid flattened coins of gum.
I turn towards the east and stand amazed,
the turrets of the ruined gable end
hold up on high the huge moon's lantern globe.
I head for home, avert my curious gaze
from stages set in lighted window frames,
and just within a stone's throw of my house
I see the moon has sailed a quarter round.
Illusion of this season – only Autumn shows
the true alignment of our streets, no grid
of squares, but pilgrims' medieval ways.

We persist in using the term 'The Kingdom of Fife'. It was a Pictish kingdom. By a stroke of chance we have a fine testimony: the extraordinary sarcophagus in the Cathedral Museum. It was discovered in 1833 when a deep grave was being dug near St Rule's Tower (the name Regulus is interchangeable). Some time during the last decade of the 500s A.D., it seems that a follower of Columba brought Christianity to this headland by the sea. You can no longer find the cave in the cliffs where the eremite dwelt. The cliffs have been eroded by the waves and have been skilfully redded up.

Riaguil known as St Rule

The north wind, gathering force, buffeted the cliffs,
lashed the settlement on the rock-ridge headland,
sent the tillers of soil, fishers of the sea
into the harbours of their stone-built huts.
Next day was still and fair, remembered long
as the day the stranger from the West arrived.
Yet stranger was the place he chose to dwell,
the cliff-face cave, east of where fresh waters
of the burn slide into the vast salt sea.
At dusk, tide out, lads playing on the scaurs,
went to help him hoist roped wood to his cave.
At fall of night and break of day, they came,
stood on the headland, held by the beauty
of his strange chants. They noted that
the wild wheeling of the gulls, the tortured
screams of lost souls, ceased. In time
the new faith cradled them. How could they know
of the grandeur that would come, the tower
touching the clouds, a mighty church, palace
for prelates, their small world a pilgrim shrine?
Thank God they never heard the cannon's blast,
nor smelt the reek of martyrs' burning flesh.

BW

The scholars have written about these early days. The legends are attractive and persistent, the sieving of hypothesis and scanty facts tentative. Ursula Hall's book on the subject St Andrew is fascinating. It seems that Acca brought the holy relics from Hexham about the year

761 to the Culdean Community of St Mary on the Rock. How did he get them? Were they really the bones of St Andrew? Three hundred years later the shrine church of St Rule was built to house them. At a lecture I attended the speaker said there was no way of knowing where the holy relics had gone at the time of the Reformation.

When Nectan, king of the Eastern Picts, sanctioned the establishment of the Roman church, the Culdee monks were supplanted by the Augustinians. In the 12th century large-scale building began: St Rule's church, the Priory, the Cathedral, chapels, houses, monasteries. Power, prosperity and fame came to this small end-of-the-road place. In 1337, 33,000 pilgrims visited St Andrews, but before two centuries had passed the winds of change had arisen; gradually they increased in strength, and St Andrews was caught up in the storms of the Reformation. In the roadway above the Castle there is a mosaic of stones making the initials of George Wishart, who on 1 March 1546 was on this spot strangled and burnt on a pyre. His words are recorded: 'This fire torments my body but in no wise abates my soul.' It is said that Cardinal Beaton watched Wishart's death from a window in the Castle. Later Beaton's corpse was strung there for all to see. The monument to the Martyrs stands high on the Bow Butts. And in the cobble stones outside the gateway to St Salvator's are the initials of Patrick Hamilton, who for six hours burnt at the stake. Beaton was told, 'If ye will burne them let them be burnt in low cellaris, for the reek of Maister Patrick Hamilton has infected as many as it blew upon.' From this infection St Leonards College, built to bolster the Catholic faith, went over to the cause for reform. And now, each year on the anniversary of Patrick Hamilton's death the students hold a service and place flowers on the spot where he died.

In April the annual Kate Kennedy procession commemorates with dignity the story of St Andrews. At two o'clock the Katharine bell of St Salvator's tolls, the great wooden gates open and St Andrew, robed but barefoot, and carrying his cross, leads the way. He is followed by the famous men who shaped and coloured the centuries. Up and down the streets the long line goes. The silence is broken by the hooves of horses and the rumble of coach wheels, and then by the shouted invective of passionate John Knox as he threatens the doom of the Catholic church. The children watch wide-eyed; they welcome the relief of the capering court jester and the drama as Archbishop Sharp is pulled from his coach and attacked. And at last the bejant chosen to be Kate Kennedy and dressed in Kate's medieval costume appears in a coach decorated with daffodils. Nowadays they call her the symbol of Spring. The legend we knew as students was this: it was the evening before the great day of the inauguration of the Kate Kennedy bell in the newly-built tower of St Salvator's chapel. Kate was staying with her uncle, Bishop Kennedy, and disgraced herself by leaving the house and taking a walk with a student. As a punishment she was to spend the next day indoors. She was to sit at a high window and might watch the ceremony from there; her uncle would able to see that she was obedient. A girl of spirit and initiative, she managed to arrange that the boyfriend had access to the house. They changed costumes; he took her place at the window and she slipped out and enjoyed the pageantry. A symbol of Spring? –was it new hope for the growing university perhaps? With that, eventually, came the emancipation of women. But women students are still battling to take part in the Kate Kennedy procession!

Chapter 2

ST ANDREWS AND THE IRVINES

One of the many books about St Andrews was published in 1970; the title is *The Avenue of Years. A Memoir of Sir James Irvine.* It was written by his wife, Lady Irvine, after his death in 1952, but sadly it is now out of print. Because of Lady Irvine's poor health their daughter Veronica completed the book. It is a portrait of a distinguished man, described in the prologue to the book thus: 'he had a genius for love, and that love, spiritual and mental, he laid with a great deal of physical effort and endurance at the feet of his Alma Mater. I have never known his inner vision fade, nor his enthusiasm that was the outcome of that vision, fail.' But the book is more than a portrait of a brilliant chemist and a great administrator; it is a love story of two important people and their family, and also a story about their love of St Andrews. It conveys the spirit of St Andrews, Town and Gown, in the first half of the twentieth century.

The family story begins in October 1899 when Mabel Williams of Dunmurry, Co. Antrim, went to Leipzig to study piano and violin. She was nineteen, and was accepted as a student by the Russian pianist Siloti. Before long she met James Irvine who was then twenty-two. As a young man he had had gone from his home in Glasgow to work in the Chemistry Department at St Andrews University. Professor Purdie marked him as having great promise and encouraged him to take a degree in Chemistry. In 1899 James Irvine was in Leipzig on an 1851 Exhibition Scholarship to work as a research chemist under Wislicenus.

The friendship between Mabel Williams and Jim Irvine blossomed; they shared a love of music and enjoyed going to concerts, boating, and walking. She writes that before her year in Leipzig was over, it was clear that their love was deep. But it was some time before they could become officially engaged, and even then they had a long wait – five years of separation except for his visits to her family and her holidays with his. At that time a man did not marry until he could provide for his wife. Mabel returned to her home at Dunmurry; she played in a string quartet and in the Belfast Philharmonic Orchestra. James Irvine completed his second year at Leipzig and returned to St Andrews as assistant to Professor Purdie.

St Andrews at the Turn of the Century

In February 1905 Mabel Williams was invited to St Andrews to stay with Professor and Mrs Purdie at their home at 14 South Street. 'Jim showed me St Andrews' she wrote, '… all was as beautiful as he had promised me'.

I try to imagine her first impressions of St Andrews. It was a quiet and peaceful place, small and compact. The setting is superb, the north side flanked by the sea, to the east the old harbour and the beach, and to the west the links and a mile-long stretch of golden sands. To the south fertile fields of farms run up to the cradling rim of the slopes. Now, nearly a hundred years later, apart from the clutter of traffic, South Street and North Street remain impressive and dignified, and are unusually wide. Walking from west to east down either street, the ruins of the massive Cathedral on which they converge loom up. Today the sight of the ruins seems to me to be like a gigantic stage set – by day, lit up by the sun, at night by discreet floodlighting. It is incredible that so much remains, for it was neglected for centuries after the Reformation, battered by rain and gales, and used as a quarry by builders. Yet the east gable, the south wall and part of the west gable tower stand staunch against the sky, together with the tower of the church of St

Rule, and other fragments of the cathedral and priory: evidence of the one-time splendour and the stormy history of St Andrews.

South Street is still lined with lime trees. The planting of trees was initiated by John Milne in 1878, and by 1894 he had achieved his goal of further tree plantings in North Street, Market Street and The Scores. So by 1905 – the year we are considering – the main streets were wide, treed avenues. We read in Milne's obituary 'the task to him was a labour of love; and as long as the trees spread their green branches over our streets his name will be honoured by our residents'. It was John Milne, eminent architect, town councillor for twenty-five years, who – together with the builder John McIntosh – planned and successfully executed the Lade Braes walk. It has been described as a 'green lung to the city' and has been lovingly tended through the years.

Miss Williams must have been impressed by the surroundings at 14 South Street: across the road is The Roundel, part sixteenth-century with seventeenth-century remodellings, its round staircase tower jutting out into the pavement. Near the Purdie's house is the holiday lodging of Mary Queen of Scots (it is now the library of St Leonard's School). Running westward is the row of grand town houses once owned by gentry and by wealthy merchants, each house with its own long narrow rigg. They tower up, plain built from local stone from Strathkinness Muir and Hill of Nydie, which, when lit by the sun, is honey coloured. The fabric of many of the old houses in the town came from the 'quarry' provided by the deserted Cathedral and Castle walls. There are half a dozen houses in North and South Street where parts date from as early as the fifteenth century. St John's House (67-69 South Street) is now thought to be one of the oldest town houses standing in Scotland; it was built about 1450 for a draper of the town, William Arthur, to replace an earlier timber house. But in 1905 its appearance would not have been so striking as it is today. (The University acquired the house in 1970, obtained a grant from the Pilgrim Trust and, under the direction of the eminent local architect Mr W. Murray Jack, a reconstruction took place. Harl, strapping and plaster were removed from the walls and an excavation was carried out in the courtyard. It was then possible to discover its architectural history and its connection with the Knights of St John.)

Half-way along, the south side of the street is dominated by the Town Hall, and the north side by Holy Trinity, the church built for the townsfolk in 1411, and drastically reconstructed by Robert Balfour in 1798-1800. (Two years after the marriage of the Irvines, MacGregor Chalmers transformed Holy Trinity into what John Gifford in *The Buildings of Scotland: Fife* describes as 'the beau ideal of a late medieval burgh church'.) The old medieval custom is still kept – every evening at eight o'clock the Holy Trinity bell 'sounds the knell of parting day'.

Other houses in South Street are of the sixteenth, seventeenth and eighteenth centuries, with some Victorian and Edwardian reconstructions and replacements. The old houses are slate-roofed, the windows long and narrow, all in dignified proportion. Handsome doorways open on to wide pavements. Among the tall houses there remains an occasional small pantiled eighteenth-century cottage. Madras College was designed by William Burn in the style of a Jacobean manor and built in 1832-34. Dr Andrew Bell, who was the son of a St Andrews hairdresser, left a legacy of £50,000 for its foundation. It is set well back from the street frontage and the ruin of a chapel of Blackfriars Monastery. Yet when it was first built there were those who strongly objected to it.

As a guest of the Purdies, Miss Williams would have been introduced to the long history of St Andrews by viewing the ruins, the religious precinct of the Priory, the Cathedral and the tower, 108 feet (30 m) high, of the first parish church, St Rule, and in the Scores the Castle which was once the fortified Palace of the Bishops. The city was not walled, but had ports of entry; two of these remain. In the early sixteenth century Priors John and Patrick Hepburn reconstructed a fourteenth-century wall; they enclosed the thirty-acre ecclesiastical precinct with a defensive wall twenty feet high and three feet thick, a mile in circumference and with sixteen towers, thirteen of which remain. The wall varies in width along the top and I have heard it said that there was once a parapet walk for eminent visitors to view the extensive site. (However, as schoolboys, John di Folco and a friend walked the top of the wall, and they were unable to walk side by side.)

On her first visit the Purdie's guest would surely be shown St Mary's and the old University library, and St Salvator's chapel, the United College – and perhaps 'Jim's chemistry lab'. I like to think that the sun shone, and that the two of them went down the little hill to the harbour, and along the east sands past the fields of St Nicholas farm, up the slope to the cliff walk. But it was February; more likely the cliff walk was first taken on a fine summer day when they were settled here.

The young couple's wedding was to take place in early June, and they were looking for a house. Mrs Purdie had said, 'It does not matter where you live in St Andrews.' There was a flat above a butcher's shop, but to Mabel's relief it was not suitable. There was a large house in Queens Gardens, about which she writes: 'the only bath in the house was in the floor of a dressing room, where one supposed a ring would have to be lifted, and a trap door opened, before the bath appeared below the level of the floor. Jim would have none of it. ... the whole town was so full of nooks and crannies and twisting lanes and doors in walls, that I felt sure I should find the ideal cottage with a modern bathroom and a quiet garden, at every corner I turned.' By the time her stay was over they had not found a house. 'Everyone' said Jim, 'has lived in St Andrews for sixty years. No-one ever leaves St Andrews until he must.' This was true in his case; he had already refused an offer of a post elsewhere, and was to decline others over the coming years. He said that when he first came to the city as a boy, 'I stood amazed under St Salvator's Tower and I knew I had come home.'

The Irvines: Early Married Life, and Work

After the wedding and a honeymoon in Ireland, the Irvines travelled to St Andrews to a small furnished house, near the Chemistry labs, which they rented as a temporary home. Their wedding presents were stored in the cellar of the lab, and her wedding dress lay on the bed in the little spare bedroom. But very soon they were able to settle down; they bought and furnished what she describes as 'a newly-built cheerful house' on the road to Strathkinness 'with big windows that looked out on the University playing-fields... the woods of Strathtyrum, the links, the sands, the white-edged waters of the bay, the hills of Angus and the peaks of the Grampians.'

She writes: '... that early life in St Andrews had an atmosphere which I find hard to define; calm, cultured, leisured and secure; both Town and University contained a small circle, and, in the large houses in the surrounding county, an unusual number of distinguished and interesting people. ... Young lecturers and elderly professors met on terms of easy intimacy and friendly argument.' She recalls the Sunday afternoon winter tea parties behind drawn curtains and before blazing fires; sometimes there was music. There was a custom in those days: at dinner parties, 'for six months a bride took precedence over every other guest no matter what her rank. ... it was considered a compliment to one's hostess to wear one's wedding gown.' Because of this the Irvines would order a cab instead of walking (which they preferred and enjoyed).

There must have been many dinner parties, for one evening Jim said, 'That wedding dress of yours has cost me a fortune in cabs.' Mrs Beatrice Copson, who came here as a bride in 1931, even now remembers her apprehension at the prospect of dining at University House and taking the seat of honour. Dr and Mrs Copson had a house built in Buchanan Gardens west of the first home of the Irvines. She recalls the strict etiquette of returning calls: the visit must be made between quarter past three and quarter to four; one of the wife's and two of the husband's visiting cards were to be placed on the waiting silver salver. An invitation to stay to tea was to be graciously declined.

In her book Lady Irvine describes how they walked down to the lab in the evenings, and 'Jim would explain his research'. 'Our pleasures were simple, but Jim could make everything we did exciting. Nothing was ever dull – we rode our bicycles out into the depths of Fife, that lovely county with its long lines of low hills against the sky, its wooded dells, its white-washed red-roofed farmhouses, its prosperous fields sloping down to the blue waters of the North Sea.' And there was music; Lady Irvine wrote that her husband had a good voice and would entertain the company by singing in German parts from Wagner operas, at the same time conducting an imaginary orchestra, and they often played at student functions.'

In 1909 Professor Purdie retired and the Court unanimously appointed James Colquhoun Irvine to the Chair of Chemistry. He was thirty-two. So the Irvines bought Edgecliffe, a three-storey plus basement part of a double-villa on the Scores, just across the road from the Chemistry labs. It had, to her mind, 'a quite hideous exterior'. It was designed by George Rae and built in 1864-66: it is described by John Gifford as 'crow stepped, machicolated with turrets corbelled diagonally across the corners of the gabled end bays'. I myself enjoy gazing at this lofty and pleasing fantasy; I like its elaborate symmetry. In the depth of winter the afternoon sun lights up the top two floors. The walk along the Scores today is still a peaceful one, and the architecture of the large Victorian stone-built houses and hotels fascinating. To the west, and next to Edgecliffe, is the Principal's House, then called Scores House, designed by John Starforth of Edinburgh, and built in the same two years as Edgecliffe. (Strange to think that for centuries the Scores were feued out in grazing strips, and that this land by the cliffs and on the south side of the Scores, apart from The Whaum, was not developed until after 1860.)

This is what Lady Irvine says in her book about their move to Edgecliffe (they changed the name to Edgecliff), after the removal men had gone: 'Mary [their Irish maid] brought us tea and hot buttered toast, and as we sat in our big easy chairs, relaxed and at peace, a strange thing happened. Down the chimney, over the red fire flames, fluttered a large white butterfly. It hovered over our heads and once round the warm room, then vanished into the cavern of the night. The gale shrieked round the house and Jim said, "It is a good omen."' And indeed they were very happy there; their daughter Veronica was born in1911, their son Nigel in 1914, and their second daughter Felicity in 1920.

I must also quote what she writes about the University at that time.

> There existed a feeling that was called "the spirit of St Andrews" – it was a real and a good thing. It bound together the small band of students who realised that if their numbers were few, the knowledge they were seeking had no boundaries. They wrote poetry about it – they sang about it – the songs from the Scarlet Gown were worth singing. It was called the Singing University. They were proud of their red gowns, and about the grey streets, or clustered in the deep embrasure of the Castle windows, or in a long line down the pier on a Sunday morning after Chapel service, or filling the chapel, the scarlet gown always looked magnificent.

The Town and its Architecture in the Nineteenth Century

The Irvines settled down to their married life at a good time for St Andrews. It seems necessary to look back briefly, first of all at what may be called 'The City', or 'The Royal Burgh', or simply 'The Town'. In the preceding sixty years St Andrews had been lifted out of the depression into which it had slumped. The man who played an important part in this change was Hugh Lyon Playfair. He was a student here when his father was Principal of the United College. In 1804 he joined the Army as a volunteer, and the next year was posted to India where he proved to be an excellent administrator and won high honours. In 1834 he returned to St Andrews with his wife and family and was soon involved in the affairs of golf and of the town. He became Provost in 1842 and in his vigorous way set to work 'to bring cleanliness and order', albeit somewhat too sweepingly as regards some old buildings. Under his administration the royal burgh grew and prospered, apart from a dip in the 1870s due to an agricultural depression. The old Tolbooth in Market Street was demolished, and the new Town Hall was built in 1858-61. The Council chose the plans of an Edinburgh architect, J. Anderson Hamilton. John Gifford describes the design as 'suppressing some of his usual exuberance, baronial with a Flemish flavour'. When I first saw it I was amazed that such a building was on a street corner, and not standing importantly in a square.

The railway branch line from Leuchars to St Andrews was set up in 1850; the first steam train drew into the original St Andrews station in 1852. Gradually St Andrews became an important watering and golfing place. One by one hotels and houses and terraces were built to accommodate the golfing and seaside visitors, and the increasing number of well-to-do, and in some cases distinguished, people who came here to retire. The population grew steadily from 3000 in the late eighteenth century to 7000 in 1914. To summarise briefly the beginnings of the nineteenth-century developments: on Provost Playfair's instigation, South Bell Street of 1840-44, and – from an overall plan by George Rae – North Bell Street of 1845-58 (now Greyfriars Garden) were designed to link the three main streets. George Rae was a native of St Andrews, and was a wright by trade; he was recorded as an architect in 1844 and acted as adviser to Provost Playfair and the Town Council over South Bell Street, and also Playfair Terrace, and Gillespie Terrace. He was a member of the Town Council from 1851 to 1864.

In 1846 James Hope bought a field known as Colonel Holcroft's Park lying between the wast end of Market Street and North Street. He had an overall plan drawn up by John Chesser to which feuars were obliged to adhere. It is a rather special precinct which resembles parts of the Edinburgh New Town. With a central garden, three terraces of elegant post-Georgian houses were built: Abbotsford Crescent, Howard Place (a convex crescent) and Hope Street. Building began in 1860 but was not completed until the 1890s. Peddie and Kinnear's Hope Park Church was built in 1864.

Queens Gardens, a fine post-Georgian terrace of houses of polished ashlar, was also completed by 1864. The Town Hall is on the South Street corner; impressive number 2 was designed by David Rhind for the Commercial Bank. Plot after plot was sold, each house having its own garden across the road; this idea came from John Milne who was involved in the scheme. The first floor drawing-rooms face west: I remember the angled mirrors which were fitted outside the drawing room windows, so that the occupants could see who was at the front door, or who was passing by. I used to be puzzled by the strange streaky black scorings on the exterior walls some feet up, then it was explained to me that the coalman would rest his sack of coal against the wall before tipping the contents down the hole and chute to the cellar. The carts of Rutherford Grubb and Sons were an essential part of everyday life. Queens Gardens has style – even the cast iron covers of the coal-holes have intricate designs.

To the west of the town centre, Kinburn House (now St Andrews Museum and Park) was built in 1846 for Dr John Buddo. It has been ascribed to John Milne, but this is considered doubtful. John Gifford describes it as 'a castellated bedstead'! Walls still surround the large garden, and in the wall opposite the present bus station there remains a handsome gateway, now bricked up. Kinburn Terrace was built in 1860 and Kinburn Hotel (Kinburn Castle) twenty years later.

Another important event was the founding of the St Andrews School for Girls in 1877. The buildings of the old college of St

Leonards had been bought by Professor Robert Watson in 1772 and the main south range converted into houses. In 1881 these were bought by the governors of St Andrews School; two years later the school moved in, and changed its name to St Leonards School. It flourished and brought credit to St Andrews. Bishopshall had been erected by the University in 1867 as a students' residence, and was bought by the School as its first boarding house. As the school numbers increased other boarding houses were acquired, or built down the Pends and down Abbey Walk.

So when the Irvines moved to their first house on the Strathkinness road (now Buchanan Gardens), it was to a west suburb which was being developed. Walking into town they would pass many recently built houses. Even in the town centre there were buildings less than half a century old. The changes had begun and rolled on, giving St Andrews a fine array of Victorian and Edwardian buildings. The definitive book on the subject is *Building for a New Age: The Architects of Victorian and Edwardian St Andrews*, a Crawford Centre publication of 1984. It was edited by Dr John Frew of the University Department of Art History and is a collection of articles by Dr Frew, Dr Ronald Cant and members of the Department of Art History. Each section deals with a local architect or the partners in a practice – their background, training, style and contributions. There is also a section on buildings by non-local architects who received comparatively few single, but important, commissions. Throughout the Victorian and Edwardian period St Andrews' architects designed new churches, hotels and houses locally and elsewhere in Fife, and supervised the rebuilding and renovating and the extensions to town houses. In *Building for a New Age* the dated documented work and attributed work of each architect are listed. As the Dean of Guild Register of Plans does not survive before 1894, this involved some useful research, which is continuing. In only two cases – the practice of Gillespie and Scott and that of David Henry – are there complete records.

Some readers may enjoy walking round parts of the old town and the 'new' suburbs, trying to distinguish the architectural styles. Appendix I lists some of the interesting houses and other buildings. Wander along these streets and gaze in wonder at these solemn stone houses, each with a different character, round towers, square towers, turrets, stout chimney stacks (some highly ornamented) with rows of peach-coloured chimney pots; finials of carved stone or wrought iron; single, double and triple sets of windows, bow windows, bay windows, oriel windows, pierced stone balconies, ornamental shields.

Between 1895 and 1905 Murray Park was a large-scale speculative venture of terraced houses, with John Milne's work prominent. Jesse Hall trained as a stone mason and became Clerk of Works to William Nixon in Edinburgh. He first came to St Andrews to supervise work on the completion of the new buildings at United College. He returned in 1850 having accepted the post of Manager of the Gas Company. His first notable work was the Congregational Church in Bell Street in 1854 (this was demolished in 1981). He designed important houses on the Scores. In 1862 David Henry, who had a first trained as a cabinet-maker and then had a full architectural training in Edinburgh, joined him as assistant and became a partner in 1874. Dr Cant describes his small double villas as perhaps the most successful of his domestic commissions. He refers to 'the turreted corner compositions, which Milne designed in a loose baronial style, as a favourite formula', and gives the example of 1 Rose Lane in South Street. If you look at such corner buildings in the main streets, you will marvel at the uplift and importance they give – for example Gillespie and Scott's 80 Market Street (1892-3) which I remember as W.C. Henderson's printing works. The roof heights in Market Street vary more than elsewhere in the town, and it is easier here to work out which are old and which are later buildings.

As for the suburbs, the West Port was the gateway to St Andrews from the west. Outside it the Argyle suburb with its two farms and eighteenth-century cottages was not developed until the end of the nineteenth century, apart from the David Henry's splendid Gibson Hospital dated 1881. Handsome villas in Kennedy Gardens (the Rathelpie Farm area) were built for clients from 1860 onwards. Building continued into Wardlaw Gardens and Donaldson Gardens. From Argyle Street to the west there were green field sites and scope for architects and builders. Commissions for large houses with large gardens adjoining the Lade Braes were given to chosen architects: Balnacarron in 1900, Robert Lorimer's handsome Wayside in 1901-4, Hepburn Hall in 1906. The firm of Gillespie and Scott was responsible for many single and double villas, large and small. By 1914 the output of this practice had far surpassed that of any other in the town. It was responsible for University Hall off Kennedy Gardens and the Bute Medical Building at Greenside Place. This practice continued to thrive in the twentieth century under Michael and Hunter Scott, the sons of Alfred Scott. But gradually fewer and fewer commissions came in for firms in St Andrews. (The reason was that the developers arrived.)

The University in the Nineteenth and Early Twentieth Centuries

The University had faced difficult times in the nineteenth century. In 1876 the student numbers had dropped to one hundred and thirty, and the financial situation made it scarcely viable. In 1883 University College Dundee was founded, largely from money given by Mary Ann Baxter of Balgavies. A plan was put forward to move the entire University of St Andrews to Dundee. Professor James Donaldson, who became Senior Principal at St Andrews in 1886 (and was the first holder of the new office of Principal in 1890), set to work to strengthen what was here. He began to implement suggestions from the 1878 Report of the Royal Commission of Inquiry into the universities of Scotland. The Universities

(Scotland) Act of 1889 clearly envisaged the continuation of St Andrews in some kind of association with University College, Dundee. The framing of an agreement between St Andrews and Dundee was assigned by the Commissioners to the University Court and the College Council. A scheme of affiliation was hammered out. There were many difficulties: a strong opposition party included Lord Bute. It was necessary to resort to litigation. In 1896 the House of Lords found the union valid, and it came into effect the next year; University College Dundee was incorporated into St Andrews University. Each part would specialise in the subjects it was best fitted for, and there should be as little duplication as possible. The composition of the Court was altered and its powers increased. Whatever the later repercussions, this move saved St Andrews, and for the time being strengthened both parties. In 1898, a law school and a 'Conjoint Medical School' were established in Dundee, and in St Andrews chairs of physiology and anatomy were founded so that medical students spent two years in St Andrews. New orders of degrees were created, honours degrees introduced, and advanced degrees in the arts and science established. Lectureships in Botany, French, German, Political Economy and History were instituted.

These events took place in the early years of James Irvine's career and must have been involving and encouraging. Slowly the numbers of students rose. Women had been attending the University since 1877. In fact the first woman to qualify as a medical practitioner in Britain, Elizabeth Garrett, matriculated at St Andrews in 1862, but her enrolment was declared illegal by the Senate. The University introduced the L.L.A. (Lady Literate in Arts) scheme which led to the eventual admission of women to full membership. This policy saw their numbers increase. The first residence for women students, University Hall, designed by James Gillespie and Scott, was built 1895-6 and extended in 1910-11. The east end of Abbotsford Crescent, known as Chattan House, was opened in 1921 as a Hall of Residence for Men;

but after St Salvator's Hall was completed in 1930 Chattan became a second residence for women. Eventually the whole of the Crescent was obtained, and the residence was renamed McIntosh Hall. In North Street the Men's Union was established in the house known as that of the Admirable Crichton. A Women's Union, the gift of Mrs Andrew Carnegie, was opened in the adjacent Georgian Terrace.

Generous gifts were made to the University. The bequest of £100,000 by David Berry on behalf of his brother, Alexander Berry a former student, was well timed and improved the situation when it was at its worst. Lord Bute gave the Bute Medical Building, designed by Gillespie and Scott and built in 1897-99. Mrs Bell-Pettigrew gave a Museum adjacent to the Bute. Andrew Carnegie, Rector in 1902, gave £10,000 'to build a new library for beloved St Andrews'. And so the detached south addition to the old South Street library was extended in 1907-9 by Robert Lorimer. The University playing fields were also donated by Andrew Carnegie. Chemistry and Physics laboratories were erected near the United College. After 1901 regular grants came from the Carnegie Trust, and the Government provided increasing funds. The University attracted professors of the calibre of Butler, Menzies, Stout, Lindsay, Burnet, Purdie, McIntosh and D'Arcy Thompson.

Principal Donaldson died in 1915. Dr Cant wrote of him: 'In many respects he was ideally suited to guide the University through the troubled period of change. He had a wide appreciation and understanding of the field of education as a whole. As an administrator he was shrewd, patient far-sighted. ... he moved through all this hurrying and difficult period of change with remarkable sureness and a no less remarkable measure of success.'

Surely to the Irvines it was a hopeful cheerful place. There was much to rejoice in when the Five Hundredth Anniversary of the third oldest university in Britain was celebrated in September 1911. The occasion is described by Lady Irvine in her book.

> The last weeks of preparation passed. The guests of the University flowed into the little city from all Airts and Parts; like pilgrims visiting a shrine, they came on a solemn mission. In the warm September sunshine old friends met and greeted each other, and strangers greeted each other and met like old friends. One felt it in the lambent air, they had come to rejoice with the Masters of the College that here on a rocky promontory above the wild waters of northern sea the lamp of learning had burned for five centuries.
>
> In gowns of scarlet and blue and purple and amaranth, the scholars from all over the world strolled down the wide streets in deep converse... Under the arc of pale-blue sky the towers looked down on pageantry and pomp... This had been seen in St Andrews before, this was a renewal of ancient glories. Every house opened its hospitable doors and welcomed the maximum number of guests and every hotel was full.

She writes that the first of the two greatest occasions was the service of Thanksgiving in Holy Trinity, which had been recently renovated under the leadership of the Reverend Dr Patrick Playfair. The other highlight was the Address given by the Rector of the University, Lord Rosebery.

> I had never before listened to an orator and now for the first time in my life I realised the power of the spoken word. The cadences of his beautiful voice, the intonation that illuminated and never clouded the meaning, the dramatic emphasis, the historic and imaginative picture he drew of the passing of the centuries in Scotland, all held his audience spellbound.

The participants and audience were no doubt rejoicing that the

University had steadily gained in strength. To those who had been involved in the battle for survival it must have been a moving event, a time of thanksgiving. Ending her account Lady Irvine writes: 'There was a new look of determination and inflexible purpose on Jim's face and no one knew, except perhaps the very wise, that their leader was in their midst.'

She also tells a story which brings us down to earth and gives a different point of view. 'And in the train as it circled the links and the bay, one visiting golfer said to his companion as he looked back at the towers above the cliff: "Go-ahead little place, St Andrews, I hear they have got a university there now."'

Professor Irvine's Research

After three years in the Chair of Chemistry, Professor Irvine was elected Dean of the Faculty of Science, and the next year became Assessor of the Senatus on the University Court. His research into the compositions of sugars was described as pioneer work, blazing a trail, and through it the St Andrews School of Chemistry consolidated its international reputation. The research had to be set aside when the war came. In 1916 a Government department was formed to organise scientific and industrial research and to be responsible for the expenditure of Government money; Professor Irvine served on the Advisory Council. The laboratory turned to making materials needed for Army bacteriology. They had swift success in discovering methods to produce dulcitol. They then turned to the production of inulin and fructose from dahlia tubers. By 1916 there was a desperate need for novocain. Lady Irvine quotes from notes made by Sir James: 'preparation known at first stage easy. Second stage difficult. 40 universities and colleges to be involved.' Here again the work at St Andrews was very successful.

Then came the use of chlorine gas by the Germans. Lady Irvine writes, 'To a man of Jim's sensibilities and deep feeling it was a severe blow to be forced to turn his attention from the science of healing to 'the science of destruction'. Yet in his notes he wrote "An end to suspense when the decision was taken to retaliate. No alternative but surrender".' She describes the strain and unhappiness about the work on mustard gas and its use. 'He felt that the science he loved was being turned by man's stupidity and cleverness to uses contrary to God's law and contrary to any human ethical standard.' But later, 'Jim saw the last war [1939-45] as a physicist's war more terrible than the chemist's war of 1914-18. The sadness about the use to which science has been put haunted Jim for the rest of his life.'

Irvine as Principal of the University

Principal Donaldson had been succeeded by Principal John Herkless who saw the University through the difficult war years. He died in 1919. Professor Irvine was deeply involved in his research, his teaching and his regular meetings in London. From the book we learn that when the possibility of his being nominated for Principal arose he was reluctant about giving up his research. But his wife writes: 'On December 8th there was a letter from the Scottish Secretary in the afternoon mail telling Jim he had decided to forward his name to the King for appointment to the office of Principal of the University of St Andrews. His commission was dated l January 1921. From this time to the end of his life Jim put the University first, before all else, whatever it entailed of effort, mental and physical.' At this time there were eight hundred students. His idea was to build the numbers to not more than two thousand.

And so in May the Irvine family moved into University House which was to be their home for the next thirty-two years. In the course of time, Veronica and Nigel took degrees at St Andrews University.

Lady Irvine writes: 'Looking back I am struck by the fact that Jim never failed anyone. There was a strange completeness about him that unobtrusively planned and carried out what might be expected of him. From his diaries the pattern of his life emerges, the normal inevitable work of a conscientious Principal: meetings of the Court and the Senatus, of the College in Dundee, of the Carnegie Trust in Edinburgh, and of the Department of Scientific and Industrial Research in London. Each week besprinkled with committee meetings, each day also had interviews with members of the Senate, the Deans of Faculties or Junior staff, and undergraduates who had problems.'

There is no doubt that his work as Principal was very demanding and that he never spared himself. Gradually the number of his commitments increased, but he somehow made time to deal with students personally. I was told many years later by a man, who had been a student in our year, that he made an appointment to see the Principal at a time when his family was no longer able to fund him. Sir James made out a cheque from his personal account, telling him this was a gift, not to be repaid or to be mentioned to anyone. Since then I have heard of similar situations when he considered problems of students and gave wise advice and help. Recently I was shown a letter from 'J.C. Irvine' to someone who had also been a medical student. In small meticulous handwriting the Principal comments in detail on a student diary the S.R.C. had brought out, congratulating them on the achievement and discussing it in detail. Little wonder that Lady Irvine writes, 'It is difficult to see when and how he dealt with his correspondence. He had a clever and devoted private secretary, ready to work all hours. He also brought back each evening to his study a bulging briefcase, so all letters were answered, though it might be two in the morning.' She tells us how he went to the rugby matches if the first XV was playing at home and tried to take an interest in all the student activities.

In March 1923 he made his first Journey (on the S.S. Majestic) to the United States to attend the opening of the Sterling Laboratories at

Yale. This was the beginning of a regular series of visits overseas; in less than twenty years he visited the United States and Canada eighteen times, always at the invitation of universities or learned societies or at the request of the Commonwealth Fund, and made many friends. Whenever he was away he wrote home every day. Lady Irvine strongly repudiates an insinuation made in this period – that money was given to the University through his seeking it. 'He was too sensitive and too proud to approach his friends with hat in hand and ulterior motives in his head, begging, even for his beloved University of St Andrews.' The money came, she writes, because he stuck to his vision for St Andrews, and she quotes from a speech he made:

> One whose academic allegiance lay elsewhere has described St Andrews as the 'oldest, the smallest, the most romantic of the Scottish Universities', and my hope is that no other description will ever be applied to it. 'The oldest' – that cannot be taken from us. 'The smallest' – therein lies our strength and we must conserve it. 'The most romantic' – we must preserve it because it is threatened – I plead for the place to be saved for Scotland.

In 1927 Edward S. Harkness of New York made the generous gift to the University of £100,000. He was a close friend of the Principal and supported Irvine in his plans to restore the residential system. The large sum was invested in Irvine personally, to be devoted to building a Hall of Residence for men students and for founding scholarships, and for the renovation of St Salvator's Chapel. The first section of St Salvator's Hall was opened in 1930, and when it was completed in 1940 accommodated 130 students. The bursary scholarships were first awarded in 1927. Lady Irvine quotes from a letter her husband wrote to her: 'Clearly we are getting more men than before, and we are getting better quality. … In a few years time the general effect on the

University will be profound, and the introduction of the Regent system will do the rest. Fresh hope for the place has stirred within me.' But this was not the end of the generosity of Dr Harkness. Lady Irvine writes: 'In 1928 he visualised a central fund in London to be administered by Trustees, and an organisation having complete independence.' This came to fruition with the founding of the Pilgrim Trust; the Trustees of the new foundation were Lord Macmillan (who was chairman for eighteen years), Mr Stanley Baldwin, John Buchan and James Irvine.

Lady Irvine writes of the

> early and innocent days when the Rector came and delivered an address which echoed perhaps round the world and brought honour to the university. What cared John Stuart Mill, Lord Bute, Carnegie, Avebury, Haig, Barrie, Kipling, Nansen, Grenfell or Smuts about being Chairman of the Court? They had a message to give to the young people who elected them, they gave it, and went again to their own great world. Their interest remained with us and they often revisited the university of their adoption. The weight of responsibility rested on the shoulders of the Principal and Vice Chancellor, loyally supported as he was by his friends and colleagues on Court and Senate.

She continues, 'There was magic in Barrie's Rectorial – the first Rectorial since Jim's appointment to the Principalship'. She refers to the evening before the ceremony: 'How often in years to come we waited for the great and famous to arrive, laying aside for the time being our own lives, almost, I used to think, our own personalities; for a host and hostess are part of the background, the spotlight is on the guest, which is one of the reasons why it is easier to be a good hostess than to be a good guest.'

Sir James Barrie's Rectorial was held in the Volunteer Hall. The University was badly in need of a Graduation Hall, and the Principal was delighted when he heard that his friends, Mr and Mrs James Younger of Mount Melville, offered to have one built. The Youngers commissioned the architect Paul Waterhouse to draw up the plans. When they were laid before the Court by Mr Younger they were marked with the words 'For their information not for their discussion'. We read in the book, 'for Jim with his clear ideas and determined views it needed great patience to stand by and watch the erection of a building at such tremendous cost which he considered neither suited to academic ceremony nor in its elaborate and formless architecture for its setting in the wide and ancient simplicity of North Street. One thing only Jim achieved, of some importance, that the Hall was set thirty feet back from the frontage of North Street.' His gratitude to the donors remained strong.

The Younger Hall was opened in 1929 by the Duchess of York and on the occasion she 'graciously received' an Honorary LL D from the University. Lady Irvine writes of other occasions, such as Rectorials, when distinguished guests were entertained at University House:

> … Jim was always himself, eager and interested. It was an expensive determination, this of Jim's, to put St Andrews back on the academic map, beginning in his own home, without any entertainment allowance from the University, for thirty two long years. Jim was happy doing it; we made great friendships, and we received more, far more, than we ever gave.

Lady Irvine recalls a moving event which took place when St Salvator's Chapel was being restored.

> It was proposed to remove the plaster from the interior walls and reveal the ancient original stonework. The

result was a shock to everyone for the walls were found to be broken and mutilated. This was supposed to have happened when in the eighteenth century the stone barrel roof was cut away and allowed to crash into the interior of the chapel, damaging everything in its transit.

On a day of cloud and sunshine and high wind in the spring of 1926, Jim came home at lunch time with an air of suppressed excitement. 'They are going to open Bishop Kennedy's tomb', he said to me. 'I want you to be there. We'll go up after lunch.' We stood, a little hushed group, Veronica Felicity and I, ... Jim descended the short flight of steps to the door of the vault. When it was opened the coffin broke asunder, and there, buried amidst the shifting trickling sand, lay the mortal remains of the Founder of the College. Jim stooped and lifted, cupped in his hands, the skull of the man who had prepared the way for his own work in this place. A foreman held aloft an electric bulb, the crude unshadowed light struck down into the shadows illuminating Jim's head and deeply moved face bent above the white skull. I knew he was thanking God for the life of this great man and praying for strength to carry on the work which had yet to be done. ... A little later the members of the College met in the evening dusk and by candlelight held a service as the coffin of the great Bishop was once more with dignity and reverence interred in the tomb that had been built years before.

Sir James Irvine was a man who was deeply concerned about the history of St Andrews, its traditions and its old buildings. One of his dreams was to see the restoration of St Leonards Chapel; it stood, a roofless ruin, older than the college of St Leonards which was founded in 1512. The opinion of Sir Robert Lorimer was that it would not stand restoration and would be better built anew. It was not until 1948 that the work of restoration under the architect Ian Lindsay began. The Pilgrim Trust paid for the work on the fabric, and Sir David and Lady Russell for the furbishings of the chapel. Sir James was to see the work finished, apart from the toppled bell tower; this remains undone.

By the time I arrived in St Andrews as a seventeen-year-old student, the numbers of students had risen: in 1932 the total was over 1000, with 580 in St Andrews and 430 in Dundee. The greatly respected Principal held the reins were very firmly in his hands. He had been knighted in 1925. On invitation he acted as Principal of University College Dundee from 1930-39. By the students he was affectionately known as 'Jimmy the Princ'.

Chapter 3

A STUDENT AT ST ANDREWS, 1933-1936

I was born on 12 December 1915 in a small mining village near Bishop Auckland in County Durham. My father had bought a medical practice there in 1912; he came from Kilwinning in Ayrshire, and my mother from Elgin. From the time I was eleven I was a boarder at Sunderland High School, and at seventeen was determined to leave. Our head-mistress was the admirable, scholarly, and sometimes formidable, Miss Ironside, and she had plans for me which entailed a further year at school.

It was my mother who came to the rescue. In September 1933, with enormous optimism and excitement we prepared for my departure for St Andrews University. The trunk, well packed with new clothes (chosen with care and pleasure at Binns in Darlington), was collected by the railway wagon, and went off 'Luggage in Advance'. Looking back it seems like a well organised miracle that when I reached my room in the residence at St Andrews the trunk was sitting there waiting for me.

I did not travel alone. I had been informed that I was to share a room in Afton, an annexe to University Hall, with one Elizabeth Barker of Highgate, London, also a first-year student. We had been in touch, and she came to spend two nights at my home; from the start we got along well. Unlike me, she already knew St Andrews, and was usefully railway-wise. It was a most entertaining journey. She was amazed that I did not know Edinburgh, and I was even more amazed at the sight of the Castle – and then of the Forth Railway Bridge. We disembarked at Leuchars, which was a larger model of my young brother's toy railway station, hump-backed bridge, porters, and a tiny waiting-room with a coal fire. The small steam train was waiting for us on the St Andrews branch line platform. Students piled in with a clutter of belongings. At Guard Bridge I hung out of the open window to witness what Barker described as 'the handing over of the tablet'. With the train in motion, the driver reached out to give a waiting railwayman a metal loop to which was attached a container with a key, a device called 'The Tablet' to ensure that only one train could be on the single-line track.

Then came my first glimpse of the sea, of the long stretch of golf links and the towers and spires of the city. St Andrews station, with a row of flower beds and its name spelled out in a design of flowers and shells, was a seething mob of students, bicyles, golf clubs, luggage. Barker ran up the steps at top speed, and when I emerged she had secured a cab. For cabs and horses it was, apart from the Royal Hotel horse-drawn bus. We bowled along smartly and turned into Kennedy Gardens. I was overwhelmed with the grandeur of the beautiful sandstone houses and the wide view over green sloping fields, over the links, over the sea, to the coast and the distant hills of Angus. The cab pulled up at Afton, Barker thanked and paid the cabbie and he looked at her approvingly. She was six feet one inch tall and stooped slightly; she had great charm. She was surely one of the most original of characters in her ideas and her sense of humour. She remarked that Afton would suit us very well, even though we had not been given either of the rooms which had 'The View'. Our room was on the first floor and faced west. I thought Afton was delightful; it was built in 1862 for Mr Aikman, owner of that very superior grocer's shop, Aikman and Terras. Subsequently the Everard family had owned both Afton and Rathmore. I liked the clean- cut style of Afton, but was puzzled that the handsome front door was set at an angle.

We left unpacking until later and walked along to University Hall to report to Miss Dobson, the Warden. On our left was Rathmore, the strangest house I had ever seen. Described by John Gifford as 'a wavily barge-boarded lodge which has shot upward, the height made almost ridiculous by the fourstorey tower, its ogee-headed attic windows striking a Gothic note'. 'Come on', said Barker, 'We've masses to do. You can absorb this one on the right later on – it's Westerlee'; (Gifford says, 'Milne, and Baronial with a vengeance 1865-8'). I was in a strange new world with houses which seemed like illustrations for a book of fairy tales. This was my second visit to Scotland – I had visited Elgin once when I was eleven.

University Hall was impressive. It had been built thirty-seven years before, as the first residence for women students. It was designed by local architects Gillespie and Scott, and noted by Gifford as 'pacific baronial with lots of crowsteps'. I don't remember that first brief meeting with Miss Dobson. She was an austere figure whose main aim seemed to be to guard the virginity of her students. The rules were plain; whether residing in Hall or in an annexe you must be in by ten o'clock. If for a good reason you were to be out later, then permission had to be sought. On sallying forth in the evening you must sign you name in a book in the Hall, and sign in on your return with the time. To ensure this was carried out, a rather meek elderly lady (termed Porter, but called by the students 'Snoop') was employed. She spent long boring evenings sitting near the front door, checking that the latecomers signed the correct time. I later discovered that the students who slept in a downstairs room at Hall were bothered by people pleading entry by their window. Another ruse was to get the escort with whom you had lingered, maybe on Jacob's Ladder, to ring the Porter from a nearby phone box and engage her in conversation, while you slipped in and signed an earlier time. Also employed at Hall was 'Nurse'; she knocked at every single door every morning, 'All right, Miss Anderson?', and needed a response, partly to check that nobody had died, but also, I suspect, to make sure nobody had spent the night elsewhere. At Afton and at the next-door rather grander Kinnessburn there was a senior student in charge of this and other matters.

We were soon unpacking, Barker's mother seemed to have bought bales of viyella and a dressmaker had made up a large number of dresses. Barker laid them side by side in a chest of drawers, rolled up as they had been in her trunk. We had breakfast at Afton and lunch and dinner at Hall; we always changed for dinner. It would be time to leave and Barker would be kneeling on the floor, pressing yet another dress with a small portable iron which was heated by igniting a methylated spirit tablet. I associate that smell with anxiety about being late, and sprints along Kennedy Gardens. Miss Dobson dined at a table mounted on a dais in a window recess. If you were late you had to advance before her and bow; she acknowledged this with a gracious inclination of the head. Each evening she was flanked by the three students who had received formal invitations to dine with her. This was known as 'dining high'. She showed a tremendous interest in what was going on, gently quizzing her guests, especially on the subject of romances.

Each of the tables at Hall was set for eight places, and we kept to these for dinner. We very soon got to know our fellow students in Afton and in Kinnessburn. Some of these friendships have been kept up for sixty-five years – amazing! The food was good. On Sundays we had Scotch trifle and collected cream in a bowl to use with coffee in our rooms. Every room, both at Hall and the annexes, had a coal fire; this was cleared out daily by the maid and the coal bucket refilled.

Elizabeth Barker was always known as Barker, and I became Liz. Next day after breakfast in Afton, Barker and I proceeded to North Street, to discover where the room of the hebdomadar was, so that we might register. For the first time I passed under the archway of St Salvator's chapel tower and into the Quad. The Hebdomadar's room was up a winding stone stair in an ancient building. In spite of his title, he was human and welcoming. We then had a look at the college buildings. Barker pointed to a wooden rack in the Cloisters. 'That' she said 'is called Cage. It is where you'll find a letter from an admirer – if you're lucky'. I couldn't wait. The buildings surrounding the Quad, particularly St Salvator's Chapel, seemed to me as beautiful and as venerable as those of any Cambridge College. The handsome ranges to the east and north of the quadrangle dated from 1829 and 1846. And of course Chapel was built between 1450 and 1460 and is very fine.

Our next mission was to buy second-hand bicycles. The one I chose was in need of a coat of paint so I got two tins, cream and green, and a brush. I painted my bicycle in the two colours, the centre frame green and the outer parts cream. 'Just like a lettuce sandwich', Barker said, and so it was always known as Sandwich. No locking of bicycles in those days – you propped your steed against any available wall or railing. In my second year Sandwich collapsed one morning in the Market Place. I pushed it along to Mr Duncan's shop and he said it was finished – nothing could be done with it. After lunch I left notes for all my friends telling them the news, inviting them to a funeral feast at nine that evening, and requesting them to wear suitable mourning clothes. They all arrived at dinner dressed in black. Miss Dobson (we always called her the Dob) was desperate to know who had died!

But back to my first week. The next day we went to our respective advisers of studies. In the afternoon we did some sight-seeing, including the Castle and Cathedral ruins. We all fell in love with St Andrews – with the clean wide streets, the ever-changing sea, the bright northern light flooding the old stone buildings, the green farmlands right up to the edge of the town. 'Now we'll go to the Victoria Cafe for tea', Barker said. 'It's known as Caif; it's the top place with the students.' And so it was; in fine weather the courtyard tables were soon bagged. There was a garden with a pergola covered with roses alongside the street, tubs with small trees, tables with white cloths. The waitresses wore black dresses, white aprons and head-bands to match. On each table was a three-tier electroplated stand with scones, chocolate biscuits and cakes. In elegance it surpassed Binns in Darlington!

I don't recall many of the shops, except for a grocer's called Haxton, where we bought packets of fire-lighters and fancy biscuits. The popular way of entertaining was by 'throwing coffee circles'; the guests came some time after nine o'clock in pyjamas and red gowns, and bearing mugs. My mother used to send cakes she had baked in the parcel with my clean washing. Dorothy Rattray, who, I think, was of the Rattray family, jewellers of Dundee, used to have hampers sent regularly. This seems to me now a very easy and unsophisticated way of life. What were we like? For the most part, conscientious, keen to work and to succeed, somewhat naive, law-abiding, romantic, optimistic and sentimental. We respected the traditions and wore our warm red gowns and trenchers with pride. We admired and respected the Principal, Sir James Irvine, and were confident of the increasing prestige of the University under his able and inspiring guidance. It is hard to say just how much I learned at that time about the history of the University. Certainly I knew of its beginnings, and that it was established in 1411/1413, the third oldest university in Britain, coming after Oxford and Cambridge. But I had no idea of its more recent history. From 1727 for the next hundred years the University and the city became increasingly run down. In 1747 there was an edict from the Crown Commissioners that the colleges of St Leonards and St Salvator's be united and known as The United College. Subsequently the buildings of St Leonards were sold. In 1826 a Royal Commission recommended that the buildings of United College should be reconstructed under William Reid.

It was compulsory to take five general subjects in the first two years; for my first, year I opted for English, Latin and a course termed Natural Science, which involved a term each of Zoology, Botany, and Geology. This was an option in the obligatory science course. I had some difficulty finding my way to the first Zoology class, and when I entered the lecture room the famed Professor D'Arcy Thompson was addressing the class. He stopped and indicated a seat, I murmured apologies and, my face flooded with colour, I struggled to get my Jotter from my bag. 'Now we may proceed', said the professor. I leaned sideways and copied from my neighbour's pad 'A BEAVER'.

That sounded hopeful, but it gradually dawned on me that the erudite flow could in no way be related to that animal, so I leaned the other way and copied out the mysterious word 'AMOEBA'. In the afternoon at the Zoology Practical I met my Waterloo. Try as I might I could not get any amoeba to reveal itself under my microscope. The memory of my inglorious and short-lived career in the lab at school came forcibly back to me. After the class I asked, and was given permission, to do a year's geology instead of 'Nat Sci'. I regret having attended only one lecture of 'D'Arcy's'. He was a brilliant all-round scholar. It was said that at the age of twenty-three he could have applied for any of the three vacant chairs at St Andrews, Mathematics, Classics and Zoology, being equally well qualified in these subjects. My brother, John Anderson, who came to St Andrews to do Science and Medicine in 1936 recalls that D'Arcy often brought a dead animal into the class and lectured on it. One day it was a wild duck. He drew the cantilevered Forth Bridge on the board and then with ease converted it into the skeleton of a duck. Then he sat talking, while stroking the duck which lay on his knees. Suddenly he stopped. He was glowering at a student in the front row who had fallen asleep. He hurled the duck at him and caught him full in the face. D'Arcy would sometimes look in at the dissection classes and become impatient at the clumsiness of some of the students. But when he himself showed them how to dissect a frog, strands of his long white beard got caught up in the frog's nerves. He was a tall imposing figure who was seen walking the streets wearing an Inverness cape. In his later years he carried his parrot on his shoulder. His home was in the row of seventeenth-century mansion houses on the south side of South Street, number 46. He had two very accomplished daughters, but more of them later.

Geology turned out to centre on more tangible and visible material. One snag was that we had to memorise the mineral constituents of a large number of specimens. With no training in science, I found the only way to do this was by a system of phonetics and rhymes; this served me well for the exams, but left a complete blank on the subject shortly afterwards. I remember an expedition along the East Sands, with the green fields running beside them, and on along the cliffs. We were armed with hammers and collected rock specimens. We paused at the Maiden Rock (used for practice by would-be mountaineers) and then the Rock and Spindle, and walked along to the Buddo Rock and Boarhills. This coastal walk might have been a hundred miles from civilisation – it was wild and unspoiled, and there were many seabirds (do you remember the heron near the Castle or the seals nosing up in the water?).

Professor Blyth Webster met his General English class at nine o'clock. He was handsome, debonair and immaculately dressed, always with a bow tie. We sat and scribbled and scribbled the scholarly information he propounded. Mainly, it seemed to be an analysis of the different folios of Shakespeare plays. There were no tutorials. Eventually an essay was set, and I spent a lot of time on it. It was returned some weeks later with a beta plus and not a single comment. We also studied 'Beowolf' but this struck no sparks. (It was a different matter when in 1999 Seamus Heaney read parts of his translation of Beowulf.) I found that Special English would involve a year of Anglo-Saxon with Dr Oakden, and I sat in on one of his classes. I decided not to continue with English after the first year. I discovered years later that my English teacher at school had been very disappointed. (The few regrets I have in my life are not about things I did, but about things I did not do – why did I not write to her and explain?)

General Logic – held at five o'clock – was, in contrast, a lively class. We listened with interest to the fascinating lectures given by the aptly named Dr Wisdom (his full name was John Arthur Terence Dibden Wisdom). On one occasion after the register had been taken in the customary way (Miss Anderson – adsum, and so on down the list), he looked up and said in his wry way, 'The auditory evidence does not correspond with the visual evidence. Would those who are answering for their absent friends kindly request the pleasure of their company at these lectures?' If he noticed that the attention of any student was straying, without stopping his flow of talk he would throw a piece of chalk at the culprit. He was married to an attractive young wife (I believe she was a dancer), and they lived in the house at the north-east corner of College Street. He owned a much-loved horse and spent a lot of time riding. Rumour had it that it had meals with him, and walked through the house to the garden at the back. Professors and lecturers were very good about inviting students to tea parties. Usually the party was rather formal with a magnificent spread; but I heard that with Mr Wisdom it was mugs of tea on the floor and butter to spread from the packet.

At our very first Logic class, Ailsa Mckinnon for some reason arrived wearing a hat. A third-year student, Alfred Fyffe, liked the look of her, and from the register worked out her name. Next day there was a note in Cage inviting her to tea at 'Caif'. At dinner we discussed whether she should accept – she had not been introduced to him. She decided to go, and a couple of friends said they would hang around outside Caif to see if she was all right! She certainly was; it was the start of a romance which led to a very happy marriage. (Alfred and Ailsa lived at Moonzie Manse, not twelve miles from St Andrews. And Nandy, Ailsa's room-mate, grieved as we all did on leaving St Andrews 'for ever'. But after five years she was back, married to George Johnston, Minister of Martyrs Church; they lived at Rathelpie (Martyrs Manse), Kennedy Gardens.)

To return to my first year classes. To my annoyance my qualifications for the Latin class were deemed not good enough. I had to attend two o'clock classes given by Mrs Dall, who was an excellent teacher. It meant that the day was rather spread out, but I took to working in between classes in the Science library which was very peaceful place. I have not now the faintest idea where it was, whether in the Bute building or in the Library itself (which is now the Department of Psychology).

The evenings were usually set aside for lighter entertainment. There seemed to us to be a wealth of student societies. In the 1935 editorial of the Society number of *College Echoes*, R.F. Marshall wrote about 'the multiplicity of societies: big societies, little societies, open societies, secret societies, disinterested societies and mutually philanthropic societies, independent societies and parasitic societies. Each has had a wonderful year; each has been fortunate in securing the services of very distinguished speakers, with a wonderful President who was backed up by a wonderful committee.' The reports corroborate this. There is a criticism somewhere that the Contemporary Society (which actually obtained Albert Schweitzer as a speaker) never had a speaker from among its members. In one season the Literary Club invited Professors Blyth Webster, D'Arcy Thompson, Professor Grierson of Edinburgh, R.C. Sheriff and Compton McKenzie. There were two debating Clubs, one for men and one for women. I was Convener of the latter in 1935-1936. I recall that we were given excellent hospitality at an inter-varsity debate in Aberdeen.

The Dramatic Society, which Barker and I joined immediately, was 'The Mermaid'. The main production each year took place in the Town Hall; in 1934 I had a small part in 'All the Kings Horses'. In 1935 the play was 'The Anatomist' and James Mavor (Bridie) came to see it. His comment was 'this is not the first production I have seen, and it has been by no means the worst' – a bit brusque, perhaps? In 1936 the play was 'Dear Brutus' by James Barrie. Ken Broadbent's portrayal of Lob was very moving. We were a sentimental lot. 'It is not in our stars, but in ourselves, that we are underlings' gave food for thought. We were, of course, the privileged. There was one society, a private one, showing a uniqueness and a wit which make it worthy of mention. It was called 'The Drones'. The members based their behaviour and their attitudes on characters from the books of P.G. Wodehouse. Languid, inventive and amusing, they were a balancing factor to the heartiness of the rugger, soccer, hockey and shinty men. The 'Drones' I knew best were Sidney Lockhart, alias Disney, and Errol Jackson, alias Rollo, and Robert Langlands, alias Angle, who married another student Elizabeth Brash. (Later they owned and ran

Drumtochty School in Kincardineshire.) For a time I had a warm affection for Rollo, and he was my partner at a couple of dances, so I was wounded to find that he preferred a girl with a dolly sort of face who wore a feather boa with her dance dress. There were only three men in our year who had cars: Robert Boothby, who lived with his grandparents at Mount Melville, and two of the Drones, Angle and Disney.

One of the Drones wrote an article for *College Echoes* in the style of Pepys, from which I quote.

> May lst, Taking a strolle upon the Linques this Afternoone, did see Rollo and Disney playing their customary mattch, a Pass-time they have now evidentlie perfected for there was Disney teetering along, a glass of ale in his hand, partaking before critickal shottes, with them Demure carrying a large Baskett of Botts. Apparentlie all three deeming it a verie aimiable Game tho Rollo and Demure more abstemiouslie moistening when at sundry Ts, but then Angle had not the situation under Controlle yett Judging by the score.
>
> The Philosophie lectuar doth again accost me to know my progress w Berkeley. I of course have not yett perused the fellow at all, but methought to say had red a littel. Whereupon he doth enquire my opinioun of the Riting (Plaguey inconsiderate!). I nonplussed for the nonce, but rallie brilliantly replying with nonchaulance 'Verie indifferent when compared with Plato'. Whereat he quite impressed, to my great relief, for in truth it was a wild hazard on my Part.
>
> May 18th, Dropt in to the Dancing att the Unioune this Evening, but rather a poor broode of damsels. This, howevere was nothing compared with the vile Sighte of

various Uncouth Boors in sweatie open-necked shirts, which I deemed most unmannerlie and out of place.

May 26th, Lord's Day. As usuall to the Jumbo Arms at ane quarter past Noone in Angle's coach, the Landlord telling us of some Convivialitie there the night before. In Particular he doth relate how some Dogges had laid holde of an emptie barrell and in a fitt of Exuberaunce had pitched it overe a high Wall, into a Cemeterie as it happened, and the Sexton or some Clerick doth nowe claim it hath dashed against the arm of a Marbel Angell, braking it. However it is noe Concerne of ours, and doe myself deeme it rather an apocryphall yarne and perhaps but a Trick to get the Angell rearmed, as seems all the Fashioun Nowadayes.'

The Saturday night 'impromptus' – later called 'Hops' – were held in the Diner of the Students Union. The women sat on a long row of hard chairs placed against the west wall. The men stood against the opposite wall or in a crowd at the door. When the band on the platform struck up, each man made a beeline for his chosen partner; the women looked down demurely, praying they would be claimed. We danced the popular ballroom dances of the day and also eightsomes and other reels and Strip the Willow (my favourite). Anxiety grew high as the supper dance approached. If a girl did not get a partner she got no supper. Not that the supper was much – lemonade and sandwiches and cake – but the humiliation was great. In addition, whoever was your partner for supper escorted you back to your Residence. So there were always a few who went home early in misery. A member of Staff chaperoned the Dance. How strange it seems now.

Balls were held in the Younger Hall or at the Residences – Sally's ball, University Hall Ball, Chattan Ball, and were by invitation. The larger student societies also held annual balls. The cabbies had a good trade on these occasions. When you arrived you were presented with a neat be-ribbonned programme to which was fixed a pencil. The dances, together with the names of the tunes, were listed, each with a vacant space. We stood there 'taking bookings' in a hopeful and embarrassed way. But there was no worry about the supper dance, it belonged to the one who had invited you and who would escort you home. If your programme was not full, usually one of the University Staff came to the rescue. Professor D'Arcy Thompson chose the prettiest girls and whisked them off their feet in the old-fashioned waltz. The programme consisted of several foxtrots, 'slow' or 'quick', a circle waltz, an old-fashioned waltz, a waltz country dance, a tango, two Paul Jones, all interspersed with The Dashing White Sergeant, the Eightsome Reel and Strip the Willow. The tunes of the day which I remember were 'Smoke Gets in your Eyes', 'Oh you Nasty Man', 'Bugle Call Rag', 'Miss Otis Regrets', 'I Saw Stars', 'You Are my Lucky Star', 'When I grow too Old to Dream' and 'Everything's in Rhythm with my Heart'. I must mention that by regulation there was no alcohol in the Younger Hall. The supper was similar to that at impromptus, and was carried to the balcony. Seated there with my partner at my first ball, I was very taken aback when he said, 'Now we can talk. Tell me, what is your philosophy of Life?' I played for time. 'Won't you tell me yours first?', I suggested. Fortunately, with my questions interjected, it lasted until the band struck up again. I was reprieved and he did not return to the subject on the way back to Afton.

The Cinema was at the height of its popularity; The Cinema House (built in 1913 and pulled down in 1979) and The New Cinema House were both in North Street. I remember that it was uncomfortable to have an aisle seat in the Old, as you might have a gas fire very close to you. After a film at the New, we all poured into 'Flick House Caif' for coffee and chocolate biscuits. The place hummed with talk, vibrated with happiness and romance.

Most of us played games on Saturdays. I went to Dundee to play hockey and out to Downfield on the tram. After the match and tea, in the darkness the tram charged down the hill like an iron horse, the bell clanged and the lights of the city sparkled. You were conscious of heading towards the water front spanned by the Tay Railway Bridge. Maybe, you thought, the tram would not pull up, would cast off and ring its way across the Tay. On Sundays most of us went to church or Chapel. The seats at Chapel were filled. After the service what was said to be an old tradition – the Pier Walk – took place. The men headed the procession, and we followed them (strictly no mixing of the sexes). Rounding the bollard at the end of the pier, the men ascended to the high wall; we clambered up the steps at the slighly lower level, The tradition proves to have been far more recent than was said. When the Quincentenary of the University was held in 1911, Lord Rosebery, who was Rector, arrived in his yacht and was met by the students at the end of the pier. This was the first pier walk. Dr Sawyer was conductor of the Chapel Choir, and for my first two years I was a member of it. I then resigned as I volunteered to go up to Den Head on Sunday afternoons and take the little Sunday School.

Our first event was Raisin Monday, a decorous occasion compared with what is now Raisin Weekend. Each Bejantine was allotted a senior man or senior woman – a third year student. The colour of the tassels on the women's trenchers denoted their year: first years, (Bejantines) blue, second years (Semies) crimson, and Tertians gold. Each Senior prepared a framed address, a eulogy in Latin to present to the Bejantine/Bejant on Raisin Monday in exchange for a pound of raisins. (By 1999 all this has taken on a different form. There is a Raisin Sunday, starting for many with a champagne breakfast, and a day of drinking and jollification. The first year student is taken into 'an academic family' and a new whirl of social life. I believe it is even possible to have academic grandparents. There are no lectures on the morning of Raisin Monday, and a huge crowd of strangely dressed first years – slaves, fairies, etc. – carrying receipts such as toilet seats, traffic bollards, wheelie bins, are marched to Quad by their Seniors. There a battle takes place using shaving soap containers. Recently the authorities have had to take a strict stance.)

Yet we were not blameless, and our first Raisin Monday was our last. My memory of it is that at night two or three men students climbed on the roof at Afton, and got into a pantry by a skylight. To us it was as bad as the Rape of the Sabine Women, though that was not their intent and they were easily ejected. The offence which caused the Principal to ban Raisin Monday for the next three years was that some students cut the creeper in Quad. Knowing now how deeply he felt about St Andrews and the University I can understand it.

Another custom was that the women students from Hall did an annual moonlight walk, sometime after Raisin Monday. We went 'out by Cameron and in by Grange', singing lustily. At the crossroads we performed eightsome reels. When we got back to Hall our senior students entertained us to coffee or cocoa with stacks of cakes.

St Andrews had the title then of 'The Singing University'. The Student Songbook was composed by a student who was impressed with the singing. The 'Smokers', which were held in the Men's Union Diner, were a form of ceilidh. There was community singing: some songs were sentimental, but the ones we really liked were those which went with a swing and were fun, such as 'The Wee Coupar of Fife' (we roared the chorus which sounded like 'Hey Willie Walleky, Noo John Doodle, elaine kwilashity, noo nooo noo'), 'Riding Down from Bangor', 'Clementine', 'Little Brown Jug', 'Polly Wolly Doodle', 'Yip I dee, Yip I die'. There were some talented performers – Nigel Irvine, son of the Principal, and Denny Hazlett stirred every heart with their singing and guitar rendering of 'Smoke gets in Your Eyes' and 'Night and Day'. There was even the odd old-fashioned recitation. I realise the link between Victorian and Edwardian drawing-room soirées was not broken when I think back to Tommy Gibbs singing in his lovely bass voice:

I think that I shall never see
A thing more lovely than a tree.

However, that did not apply to a song which Tommy Goss made up and sang at a Smoker (he was appropriately dressed up as Miss Dobson). It began:

I am the Warden of Hall Nursery Garden
My duty, not beauty, is what worries me
My object and credo
To stifle libido
I am the Warden you see.

The singing of students was not limited to Smokers; song broke out spontaneously on any occasion. When we were waiting before a lecture we sang, to the tune of *Venite Adoremus*:

Oh why are we waiting,
always bloody well waiting
oh why are we waiting
oh why why why?

This brings a picture to my mind of one of our young lecturers, Mr Bruce-Mitford, coming in to meet his Latin class, rather red in the face and with his wonderful boyish grin. When he took the register he would come to the adjacent names 'Miss Riggall and Miss Tickel' and would struggle to remain solemn. At the graduation in 1936, when his fiancée Margaret Herring, daughter of Professor Herring, went up to be capped MB ChB, the song 'Here Comes the Bride' was sung. (I was at a graduation recently, and how different it was. Now there is music from the enormous organ, and now there is respectful silence interpersed with regular polite clapping.)

At night small groups of men would walk down the empty streets, singing the student songs. My favourite was (sung sonorously):

As through the streets
At night we went
It might be half past ten
We fell out my friend and I
About the cube of X + Y
And made it up again
And made it up again.

Now blessings on the falling out
Between two learned men
Who fight on points which neither knows
Who fight on points which neither knows
And make it up again
And make it up again.

This was indicative of the fun, the debunking of pretentiousness, the light-hearted comradeship of those days. Because of the small numbers, we got to know almost everybody, students and staff. When the summer came, Barker and I explored the countryside on our bikes. One afternoon we went over the hill to Largo and climbed Largo Law. We had tea at the Crusoe at Lower Largo; the room upstairs had a lowish ceiling and baskets of geraniums hung from it, and I remember Barker ducking to avoid them as we made our way to a table. That day for the first of many times in my life, I stopped to look at two unsurpassed views: on the way there, above Largo, the Firth of Forth and the coast- line of the Lothians; on the way back, St Andrews seen from Cairnsmill. Such views should be sacrosanct.

When the degree exams suddenly loomed near and the library seats were filled, Barker devised a way of 'swotting'. We stayed in our room, drew the curtains to shut out tempting sunlight, and kept our eyes down. The results were satisfactory. Everybody dispersed for the long summer holidays. Barker went off to Dundee docks to embark on a merchant ship, this being a cheap way to get to London. Eight of us who travelled south by train 'bagged' a compartment at Leuchars; my wind-up black box gramophone was given a seat and we had a concert of songs from the Shows (we knew scenes from Noel Coward's 'Private Lives' off by heart). For most of us the year had been the happiest and most exciting in our lives.

During that vacation I went to stay with Barker and her aunt, Miss Lilian Barker, at the Governor's House of the Women's Borstal at Aylesbury. She was a remarkable woman with a deep understanding and compassion, together with humour, common sense and strength. Each day she made her way all round the prison; any prisoner was free to come and speak to her. The girls loved and respected her. There was a small group of older women serving life sentences, and Miss Barker had set up a system of rewards; for good behaviour, privileges could be won. Each woman had her own bed-sitting room and had managed to embellish it. While I was there this group was taken on an outing to a large heath, and Barker and I went with them. It was a glorious day and when we got to our destination we split up into small groups and picked cans and cans of blackberries. After this there was a huge spread laid out on trestle tables. We all tucked in and chatted away. In the bus going back we sang song after song. Each lot of berries was clutched firmly by its owner. Next day they would make jam or jelly or tarts. (Miss Barker – later Dame Lilian – became the first woman Governor of Holloway. After her death Barker wrote her biography.)

When we went back to St Andrews in October 1934 we all moved into University Hall, and each had our own room. I had by then decided that I would take Psychology and Philosophy as my final subjects. The Psychology department was bang up to date; its locus was the basement of the Younger Hall, and the Head of Department was Dr Oscar Oesar; he was young, dark and handsome. We admired him and enjoyed his lectures. Two lecturers took our practical sessions – Dr Pierce and his wife Dr Pallister. We found that he was easily irritated. One afternoon we were told to work in twos and given sheet of instructions. The object was to test the threshold of two-point discrimination (it has never proved particularly useful to me). The first instruction was 'Place an inkspot on the arm of your partner and then blindfold him', but there was a typing error and the 's' had been omitted. We went to Dr Pierce and I said in a helpless feminine voice, ' Please Dr Pierce, I am afraid we need help as we can't get the inkpot balanced my partner's arm.' As we hoped, he blew his top.

On the 17th of October the Rector of the University was installed. General Smuts had been elected almost three years before and had been unable to come until the very end of his term of office. On the day before the Installation a great crowd of students assembled at the West Port to see the start of the Rectorial drag and to follow it round the town. General Smuts sat high in an open carriage, smiling and handsome with his goatee beard and silver hair. He was wearing the student scarlet gown. The carriage was dragged by a team of rugger Blues. Outside Holy Trinity he descended for a short ceremony of greeting by the Provost and Magistrates. I was very struck by their robes. (Over the years I became used to these. When St Andrews lost its Town Council, and David Niven became Chairman of the local District Council, it was a sad shock to see him at this same ceremony, but without the robes of office.) We followed the procession to the Men's and the Women's Union and watched the presentations of gifts to General Smuts. Then we went to University House and crowded round to cheer when the Principal and Lady Irvine came to stand outside the door with General Smuts, Sir James Barrie and Mr Stanley Baldwin.

That evening there was a torchlight procession down the pier – the dramatic scene with gowns glowing red, and yellow torchlight reflected in the sea, the singing and our excitement and our high hopes. At two o'clock the next day, a thousand students assembled in the Quad (the Dundee students were over in force), and marched along to the Younger Hall for the Rectorial. The Principal was apprehensive, as recent rectorials had been rowdy. But the SRC had a surprise for the sort of students who had come with claxons and stink bombs. They had organised groups of 'secret police' who operated in fours and swiftly ejected any trouble makers. The singing was tremendous; at the end of each chorus there were roars of 'STAND, STAND, STAND' as any person of importance sat down, so that he or she was forced to stand up and bow.

At last the academic procession filed in, well-known members of staff two by two, and we sang:

The animals came in two by two – Hurrah, hurrah,
The elephant and the kangaroo – Hurrah, Hurrah.

Last came the janitors bearing the magnificent maces, preceding the Chancellor, Mr Baldwin, the Principal and Sir James Barrie (then Rector of Edinburgh University), and General Smuts. The maces were set in their stands. Barrie looked uncomfortable; his chair was too high for him and he sat on the edge of it and twisted his feet round the legs of the chair. He looked a sad little figure.

So the scene was set, and we rose and sang the *Gaudeamus* with heart-felt fervour. The prayer was read by Mr Baldwin, and then to a huge ovation the Rector stood. The ceremony was brief and General Smuts was resplendent in his robes. We then sang a song in Dutch, 'Sarie Marias', and he was visibly moved. He began his address 'The Future of Liberty' somewhat nervously, but a few shouted student quips made him smile. He spoke of his hopes for the future of Africa – 'may she yet find the formula of appeasement and co-operation between the white and the black'. Then he turned to the present: 'the principles in the motherlands of our European civilisation are no longer considered sacrosanct and are being challenged and even openly defied. Mankind stands perplexed and bewildered before the new situation. There is a fear, a sense of insecurity among the nations. The primeval dread of the unknown is once more upon us, and the dark forces of the past are stalking us.' He discussed the present 'political experiments' which took away individual rights and the freedom of democracy. 'Today we face a bleak world – with no clear vision of the way before us. The hard truth of the matter is that they are the most anxious and critical times which mankind has faced for many centuries'. He came to the message which suited us: 'this is a good world,' he declared, and elaborated on this theme. 'It is a world built for heroism, but also for beauty, tenderness and mercy. There is no malign fatalism which makes fools of us in our dark striving towards good. On the contrary, what is highest in us is deepest in the nature of things, and as virtue is its own reward, so life carries its sanctions and the guarantee of its own highest fulfilments and perfections. That is my ultimate credo – I remain at heart an optimist. In the events of our times I see much ground for anxiety but none for real pessimism.' He spoke then of scientific advances which would help to combat the problem of food shortage. And he was encouraging in another way: 'every new war invention is making real modern war more and more improbable', he said, and he went on to attack the new Tyranny abroad, 'the fight for human freedom is the great issue – the denial of human rights must in the long run lead to cataclysm'. He ended with the words, 'Are we going to leave a free field to those who threaten our fundamental ideals and our proudest heritage from the past? Or are we going to join in the age-long battle for the breaking of our bonds and the enlargement of our range of free choice and free action. Remembering the great appeal of Pericles which rings through the ages, let us seek our happiness in freedom and bravely do our part in hastening the coming of the great day of Freedom.'

There was a tremendous ovation. Yet his optimism was unjustified. But was he ambivalent? It seems to me now that the end part might have been a declamation at the outbreak of war. But we took away what we wanted – reassurance. Of Hitler and of Mussolini he said 'in spite of the vogue of silly drilling and strutting about in shirts of all colours there is no real war temper anywhere.' Most of us were untouched by the growing fervour of Nazis. Only one dark event came to us in our cocoon here. We had two German students living in Sally's (St Salvator's). The Police had suspicions that one of them was a Nazi spy, and he was under surveillance. He had an ugly temper, and there was an incident when he rammed a student. He boasted that he was a good boxer, and a match was arranged between him and David Douglas Hamilton, with Sergeant Stark as the referee. It was the Scot who won. Then the tale crept round that this Herr T. had picked up a cat, swung it round and brained it against a wall. Before the term was ended he was sent back to Germany.

That summer vacation I worked in the Seaman's Orphanage at Liverpool. This confirmed my plan that I should apply for a place at the Rachel McMillan Nursery School Training College in Deptford for September 1936. Most of us left after taking an ordinary degree and then did a further year of specialist training. When I returned to St Andrews for my last year, Miss Dobson asked me to be Senior Student in Afton and, although I had enjoyed my year in Hall, I was glad to accept. It meant some saving for my parents who were paying for everything. My special subjects were Philosophy and Pyschology, and I was also allowed to attend the Honours Child Psychology lectures given by Dr Oesar. The two text-books I remember were William McDougall's *Social Psychology* and Freud's *Interpretation of Dreams.* Bernard Babington Smith was in charge of our practical sessions; he was very popular and, I believe, a good tennis player.

We also studied Professor Stout's *A Manual of Psychology*. Ours was the last class to attend Professor Stout's lectures. He lectured to us not only in Philosopy but also in Psychology – a very different sort of subject from the new scientific subject being taught in the Department. We sat at a long table with the venerable professor at the end. He did not use notes; he spoke in a low, weak but always audible voice, fluently, as if he was relating an old legend. He was living in the ancient world of metaphysics and sometimes remained in it when he went out into the Quad. There are various stories about him, one told by Lady Irvine. During the first weeks of the 1914 war, one night 'Professor Taylor, the philosopher, in white tennis shoes, spectacles and the communal khaki greatcoat, with an awkwardly handled rifle, was on sentry duty outside the armoury when a small but well-loved figure wandered uncertainly down Butts Wynd. The sentry's "Halt, who goes there? Friend or foe?" brought it to a standstill, and a shaken voice replied "Oh is that you Taylor? I'm sorry I'll go round the other way." And Professor G. F. Stout beat a hasty retreat into North Street.'

It was said that one day Stout walked home with one foot in the gutter and the other on the pavement, and complained to his wife that he was going lame. Another time he was going to London and telephoned home from Leuchars to say he had forgotten where he was going. Mrs Stout told him to look at his ticket! Of course such tales accumulate, and may not be true. I myself remember being invited to dinner at the house of a Philosophy lecturer, Tony Lloyd, who was unmarried. Although he was quite young, he had the reputation of being absent-minded (obviously he was heading for a Chair). There were two other guests waiting with me at the door and, when our host eventually appeared, it was clear to us that he had forgotten all about the invitations. He gave us glasses and a bottle of wine, and disappeared into the kitchen. After a long time we became uneasy, and one of the guests went to see what was happening. He found our host sitting at the kitchen table starting to eat a meal. While cooking it, he had once again forgotten about his little party!

Barker was by now in Dundee doing Medicine. She sometimes came over and we would have a game of golf. She was full of enthusiasm for life as a medic in Dundee. She eventually became a psychiatrist.

In the first term of my last year there was a memorable event – a party for which I still have the invitation.

Ye Anglo-Saxon Convivialtie
Rollo & Disney nowe attaynynge their Yeares of
Discrettioune & Wysddone do heerebye proclaime
Merriemakyinge atte
ye Postyllioune Poste-House
ann Saint Androis Daye
& bid you with despatche bee presentt ffor ane
Spotte of Brousynge & Sluyeyuge & eeke Caperynge
& Swich-lyk atte ye 7th Houre & Haiff an Hr.
to Boote after ye Sonne hys Hyghth.

The hotel was the old Station Hotel.

I remember before the Final exams pacing up and down the Long Walk at St Mary's with Jean Alexander and arguing, not about the cube of X + Y but about a certain philosophic phrase. (Jean was later to become a social worker, to marry, and eventually to return to live in St Andrews. Here she worked to establish a Cheshire Home at Glenrothes and a new railway bridge at Leuchars junction.) At twenty, she strongly asserted that 'Whatever is is' was stupid because of course it is. I played devil's advocate.

I can picture the rows of desks in the Younger Hall, the virgin sheets of paper, the pens with nibs, the inkwells, the blotting paper, and the sunshine outside. Exam papers were described either as 'not bad' or 'foul'. And I remember the relief when it was over, and a boyfriend and I went to have coffee in the garden of Macarthurs cafe. He was John Thomson, known to all as 'Tiny' – he was very tall. (Later he became Rector of Madras College.) There was time then to go down to the harbour and paddle round in a canoe. But soon came the end of term, the Ball, and the end, to us, of 'St Andrews'. Someone wrote about the feeling in College Echoes.

Cabs?
Fiacres then?
Remember rattling over cobblestones

In Market Street
After we danced our fill?
How moonlight on the gables shone –
How quiet it was!
How you remarked how soon the night had gone,
And how I answered with a yawn
Remember still?
I said
'My father and your father and his father
His father and his father
(Rest their bones)
Had heard this sound
Wheels rattling over stones.
We are the last of all our line
To hear this sound.'
A thought profound
For two o'clock.
Such talk
Makes up the stuff of memory,
Goodbye.
Echoes are unsubstantial fare,
And ghosts are lingering everywhere
The shadows linger.
Do not fix
A sentimental gaze
On what they call the good old days.
(St Andrews 1936)

But looking back who does not feel a welcome nostalgia? And it is all the more bitter- sweet in the face of what has changed, is changing, in St Andrews. Some of us did in fact come back to live here.

West Port 1589

Renaissance Group singing on the West Sands

St Andrews from the St Andrews Bay Hotel

The St Andrews Bay Hotel from the town

The old Students' Union, North Street, 16th c, remodelled 17th c.

Town and Gown

Chapter 4

RETURN TO ST ANDREWS

Just before Christmas 1949 my sister Maryan, who had been living with us in Suffolk at Waterhall Farm, drove Penny and Susan (my daughters) and myself up the A1 to our family home in the mining village of Coundon, near Bishop Auckland in County Durham. My brother John, who was a lecturer at Glasgow University, came home and we had a good family Christmas. Then John took me to St Andrews to South View, the house on the corner of John Street and the Lade Braes which was to be my new home. Pickford's van arrived on time and all went smoothly. John and I saw the New Year in with high hopes, and then he went back to his work. My mother and the girls came up by train; Penny was nearly eleven, Susan nearly nine. The sun shone, and St Andrews was more beautiful than ever. We explored the Lade Braes Walk which in all seasons was a delight.

We had brought our current pet, Philip, a strong-minded striped cat who soon achieved minor fame by presenting us with an unusual gift: a black vole he had killed. Next door to us lived good neighbours Mr and Mrs Rogers and their son Tom, who took the corpse to the museum at Dundee where it was stuffed and exhibited. Philip caused periodic agitation at number 6 John Street, the home of three sisters, the Misses Robertson who were retired teachers. They kept vigil to see that he was safely home at night, and I was reprimanded if he was not rounded up. In April the Misses Robertson conducted a thorough spring cleaning of their home, heaving a succession of carpets and rugs on to the clothes line and beating them heartily with cane bats. Each of the sisters had two fur coats. One day Susan came rushing in from school and cried,

'Maman, Les Trois Ours sont denudés, viens voir.' I went out into the garden to see an array of the six coats on the clothes line!

Penny and Susan were pleased with their St Katharine's uniform, which was the colour of porridge. The week-day woolly caps were called 'jelly-bags'. The girls took to their new school at once and soon made friends. They liked the ease and independence of cycling to and fro twice a day. One of the Misses Robertson would be on the look-out: 'Mrs Willsher, your Penny need not think that half off and one foot *on* the pedal means she is NOT GUILTY of cycling down John Street.'

I opened my Nursery School when the St Katharine's term began. Before moving north I had found out that there was no professional preschool provision in St Andrews. By advertising in *The Citizen* my list was filled before I arrived! I added new tables and chairs to the equipment which I already owned at my nursery school in Suffolk. Through an advertisement in the paper, I bought an old-fashioned gramophone from Police Judge Fraser, a large square, mahogany box, and thrown in with the bargain was a fine selection of 78 r.p.m. records – pipe bands, brass bands and Ernest Lush's 'O for the Wings of a Dove'. The gramophone did twenty years service. The schoolroom was the large upstairs sitting-room, with a view of the southern slopes; the girls called Scooniehill 'the green hill without the city wall'. We also used the adjacent bedroom as 'the brick room and the carpentry room' (noisy activities). Each morning – weather permitting (and it usually did) – my 'little school' went out for half an hour to play on the swings and chute and roundabout in Cockshaugh Park.

Through my pupils I was very fortunate in making new friends, among them the Woodwards and the Giffords of the Spanish Department, The Milligans (George was a teacher at New Park School), Joyce and Burton Pirie of West House, Mary and Robin Adam (History Department) and later Gwen and Lionel Butler, Margaret and Terence Bruce Mitford (who had been my brother's Regent and who lived across the lane from us), Mary and David Grace of 60 South Street, Philip and Elizabeth Ouston (French

Department), Bessie and David Borwein (Mathematics Department), Kitty and Arthur Read (Professor Read's son), Biddy and Alfred Cole, Daphne and Terry Lee (Psychology Department), Phil and Margot Gribbon, and many others. Amazingly, these are now friends of fifty years' standing! And of course there was Bunty Mould of the Tom Morris House who was the great grand-daughter of 'Old Tom'. She and I played golf together, and much later went wholeheartedly into the recording of gravestones. I wrote about the happiness and fun of these ten years of nursery school at South View in various articles and in my first book *School Before Five*, published by Faber in 1959.

Back to the early 1950s: at weekends Penny, Susan and I used to cycle out into the countryside. One favourite route was up the top road to Strathkinness, down Knock Hill and to Dura Den where there were two waterfalls and where an antique shop sported an array of deers' heads, heavily antlered. Sometimes we went up to Kemback and ran up the steps to Blebo Craigs, but never managed to agree on our individual counts of the steps. In the summer, on Sundays after church at St Leonard's, we would take a picnic, cycling along the cliffs beyond the Maiden Rock to what we called 'Golden Bay'. We explored the caves, and we went to see the wreck in the Eden estuary. I remember the gripping icy cold when we bathed in the Step Rock Pool, where annual galas where held. I recall a cold summer day when my daughters insisted on bathing at the West Sands. We emerged from the sea blue-faced, and battled against a stinging sandstorm. The St Leonards schoolgirls still used the old 'Ladies Pool' to the west of the Castle; it was a spartan regime.

There were other events new to the girls such as the Kate Kennedy procession and the fund-raising parade on Charities' Day. The latter came to an end in 1960 when the floats and horses from Wilson's Argyle Street Soft Drinks factory were no longer available. Elaborate and ingenious displays by the students of each residence used to be mounted on the floats. The last of the annual Horse Parades was held in Cockshaugh Park in 1952. The ornate decorations amazed and delighted us. On 2 June 1953, the day of the Coronation, there was a fancy dress parade, and the entrants assembled in the quadrangle at Madras for the prizes to be awarded. One boy in the 11- to 13-year-old class, Angus Langlands, won a prize for his topical costume 'Mount Everest Conquered'. Led by the Pipe Band the children, one thousand in all, and their parents marched along to Cockshaugh Park where there were games, and ice-cream and lemonade. Unfortunately a bitter wind was blowing, so we soon went home and had huge hot baths. Then we visited a family called Brown, who lived in Kennedy Gardens, to watch the royal ceremony on television. (We did not have a set until 1959, or a car until 1964.) In the evening there were entertainments – the Cloister Singers, dancing, tableaux – and the day ended with the singing of 'Land of Hope and Glory' led by Baillie Fordyce. A great day.

The boundaries of the town were clearly defined. The Athol Hotel was the last town building on the road to Guardbridge. Lamond Drive bounded the town on the south. To the east and south and west, St Andrews was ringed by farms: St Nicholas, Priestden, Langlands, Auldburn, Roundhill, Claybraes, Sandyhill, Lawmill, Bogward and Lumbo. There were two firms of blacksmiths in the town. David McMillan succeeded his father at Bridge Street, then at the West Port (where the Shell garage is now), and was joined by his son Gilbert. Later 'Gibby' as he was known had to move to the east end of Market Street and latterly to Bassaguard. Mr Harvey, agricultural engineer, was at Greenside Place for many years, and he specialised in wrought iron gates. Jean, a friend of mine went to see him to ask if he would make one for her at 63 Hepburn Gardens. 'If you just take a walk up and down your road,' he said, and listed numbers of houses where he had supplied gates, 'you can see what sort of thing you fancy. And if you have any special ideas, I can incorporate them.' Jean had a grandfather who had been a miller, so she had two mill wheels in the design for her new gate.

We sledged in the field by Jacob's Ladder. In January 1952 we went up Scooniehill to sledge, and later skated on the pond at Pipelands

Road. Professor and Mrs Dickie were first-class skaters and gave the girls some advice and help. We walked along the Lade Braes to watch curling on the Law Mill Pond, and in the summer I played tennis in Kinburn Park. There were games at St Katharine's every afternoon. At one School Sports Day the Day Girls did very badly (the boarders had been coached at weekends), but 'we' did well the next year as a result of the father of one Day Girl holding some coaching sessions in Cockshaugh Park. The Headmistress of St Katharine's, Miss Ludgate, was popular with the boarders – they called her 'a good sport'. When she retired she played quite a lot of bridge, and after all these years I still hear her sayings quoted: 'One up, shut up' and 'Three noes, a fool goes'.

It was exciting to live by the sea. One is always aware of its presence, especially when the wind is strong. I recall one incident; word went round the town that a Russian vessel was aground near the Maiden Rock. People streamed along the cliffs; we were very close to the crew but the impossibility of communication was frustrating. When the tide came in, the ship floated again and they managed to get it out to sea. It brought to mind the tales of the many shipwrecks in St Andrews Bay when the sound of the canon's fire sent the citizens running to the cliffs or the east or west sands. In 1765 the five yawls of our fishing fleet were wrecked at the harbour mouth and on the rocks beyond, and twelve men were drowned while families and friends stood helpless. For a time there was no fisher fleet here, until twelve crewmen from Orkney with their two boats were persuaded to come. Only one crew settled, and their descendants were fishing until the mid-twentieth century, but latterly just for lobsters and crabs. The East Infants School at Gregory Place, which began as a one-room part-time school for the children of fishermen, was extended in 1885 under the education authorities. It closed when Langlands School opened in 1957.

The many wrecks in St Andrews Bay in the nineteeth century are described in a book by George Bruce, Provost and instigator of the Bruce Embankment. The dangers of the local waters were well known. On the 5 January 1800 the sloop 'Janet' from Macduff was in trouble off the east sands. A young student, John Honey, swam out with a rope, but got into difficulties and had to cut it. He rescued the master of the ship and three other crew men by swimming out repeatedly. His health suffered as a result of this amazing feat, and he died at the age of thirty-two. He is represented in the Kate Kennedy procession, a coiled rope over his shoulder. Many St Andreans in the early twentieth century must have thought, at times of rough seas, of the names of boats which had been wrecked: The Petrel, The Packet, The Jean, The Itinerant, The Trafalgar, The Betsy, The Elizabeth, The Woodyard, The Risborough, The Mary, The Endeavour, My Sons, Cybele, The Sutlej, The Fox, The True Blue, The Wasp, The Galatea, The Bon Accord, The Napoleon, The Oscar, The Fox. In the East Cemetery are two gravestones with the names of the crews lost in two of the wrecks, and in Boarhills Churchyard another. But sometimes lives were saved; the St Andrews lifeboat was renewed three times. The names of the dangerous rocks would have been familiar – The Burn Stools, The Long Rib, The Babet Stane, The Leckies, The Doo Craigs, The Headless Man, The Hootie Tootie – but few know them today.

The Shops

The St Andrews shops were excellent, and the shopkeepers and assistants noted for their courtesy and helpfulness. I would say this tradition has persisted, although by the end of the twentieth century there are only a few family-owned shops. Sadly many excellent businesses have gone, but some I remember well. The grocer Aikman and Terras on the corner of 165 South Street and Bell Street was unique; it was founded in 1837, but not on these premises which David Henry remodelled for the firm in 1905. It was described as 'Italian Warehouse and Wine Merchants Coffee Specialists'. One advertisement was 'Of course you drink coffee. Why not have the finest? We roast each day and pack in air-tight tins'. There was dignified ritual: the customer, seated on a chair, gave her order, and the assistant went away and returned with each separate item! These could be paid for or 'entered', and taken or 'sent round' if you wished. An alternative was that an assistant called weekly at your home and took down your order to be delivered by the van man. Ladies dressed smartly in tailor-made tweed suits, gloves and hats to go shopping. On one occasion I was in Aikman and Terras and Margaret Sommerville of Hope Street was in front of me. Across her shoulders she was wearing what was not a scarf nor a fur tippet, but a pair of joined oven gloves. I whispered to her. She looked down, snatched the article off, went into peels of laughter and said, 'Yes, I meant to baste the roast before I came out!' Aikman and Terras closed this very special shop in 1977. The shop of Mr Birrell, groceries and wines and spirits, was at 89 South Street. McFarlane the grocer was at 131 Market Street; Miss McFarlane always wore trousers, which was unusual at that time. (She was well known as a conductor of the Operatic Society's performances of Gilbert and Sullivan in the New Picture House.) This splendid shop closed down in 1977.

Our baker was J.W. MacArthur, whose bakeries were at 34 and 116 South Street, and a café was at the latter; this business had started in 1890. George MacArthur & Son's bakery was at 197 South Street. Grant Milne opened Fisher and Donaldson bakers at 13 Church Street in 1950, and his sons carry on the businesses in Church Street, at 197 South Street, and in Cupar and Dundee. They are renowned high-quality bakeries. Grant and Audrey had five sons, all of whom came to my school.

There were four or five butchers in the town in the 1950s, but only Murray Mitchell's business, founded 1928, has survived. We went to David Niven at 9 Church Street; his children David and Christine were at my school. This family was an important one in St Andrews. David held various offices on the Town Council and was then elected Provost; he was the first Chairman of the new District Council. In November 1987 he and his son David went to an investiture at Buckingham Palace. David Senior received the MBE for his services in local government, and David Junior the OBE.

Since then 'young David', an Air Vice Marshall in the RAF, has been awarded the CBE for services during the Gulf War, and he will shortly receive the CB.

George Gordon had a fish shop at 59 Market Street, and another Mr Gordon had one at 10 Church Street. At number 1 Church Street Miss Evans ('Maggie the Fish') held sway. She was a cat lover and would have a bag of scraps ready for each cat-owning customer. In spare moments she stood outside the shop, hands on her hips, white-aproned, and delivered a sometimes scathing commentary on those passers-by on the other side of the street whom she did not favour. Alistair Reid's poem in which he dwells on one of his favourite topics –the Puritanism of the Scots – surely refers to Maggie.

Scotland

It was a day peculiar to this piece of the planet
when larks rose on long thin strings of singing
and the air shifted with the shimmer of actual angels.
Greenness entered the body. The grasses
shivered with presences, and sunlight
stayed like a halo on hair and heather and hills.
Walking into town, I saw, in a radiant raincoat,
the woman from the fish-shop. 'What a day it is!'
cried I, like a sun-struck madman.
And what did she have to say for it?
Her brow grew bleak, her ancestors raged in their graves
as she spoke with ancient misery:
'We'll pay for it, we'll pay for it, we'll pay for it'.

Alistair Reid

The Stravithie dairy was at 158 South Street, but it closed in 1982 leaving St Andrews without a dairy.

Our newsagent was Mr Neil Westwood by the West Port and next to Janetta's Café. If from City Road you look high on the north-facing wall of the block of property by the Port you will see in faded painting:

'MAIN ENTRANCE TO CITY AND ORIENTAL CAFE.
LUNCHEONS TEAS AND CYCLE ACCOMMODATION'.

For some time Mario de Angelis had a pipe and tobacco shop at 207 South Street. The sweetie shop we liked is still at 96 Market Street; it was originally opened by Mrs Dodge and then taken over by her niece Mrs Burns. Mr Geddes, who had previously worked at the Maple Dairy Company, opened a confectionery and fruit shop at 100 Market Street in 1927. With his son George he branched out into a most successful delicatessen, which closed down in 1982 when George began a new career in charity work. Other local fruiterers were Mrs Main at 132 Market Street – she had a great love of flowers – and Paterson's shops. Janetta's icecream shop, still at 31 South Street, was already there in 1950.

Fletcher's had premises at 121 South Street from the early 1830s. Melville Fletcher started as bookbinders and stationers, and produced the local paper and town guides. Mr Ralph Duncan became the proprietor in 1959. The shop developed into a music, book and toy shop, but it closed in 1983 and was greatly missed. When we were talking about the shops, one lady said, 'I loved walking around Fletcher's. It was full of treasures, like an Aladdin's cave.'

The Citizen bookshop and stationers at 105-107 South Street, owned by J. & G. Innes, and still in business, was previously a Georgian tenement and was renovated and opened in 1928; the frontage is described by John Gifford as 'Tudor detail à la Liberty's'. The printing works at 80 Market Street (frontage by Gillespie and Scott) – originally A.D. Cook's – were owned by the firm of W.C. Henderson, whose shop at 19 Church Street had the title 'University Booksellers and Stationers'; its frontage and interior were remodelled by David Henry in 1886. When we knew it, Mr Jessiman and Mr Martin ran it. George Hackerson, born in 1909, was employed to deliver goods to customers; he did this in a wheelbarrow known as

'Hacky's barra'. Hacky was an orphan; a simple soul, he was liked and accepted. He was very well looked after by the family where he boarded and by his employers who gave him a new broom annually on his birthday. There is a story of Hackie saying to Principal Knox who went by as he was sweeping up, 'It's an awfy besom this ane. First the heid cam off and noo it's the haunle.' W.C. Henderson's closed in 1982.

There was no need to go far afield for clothes, and there were good shoe shops: Donaldson at 163 South Street and Hoggs Fife at 90 Market Street. Mr T.T. Fordyce, who was later Provost of St Andrews for nine years, owned drapery shops at Methil and at 65 South Street, and later at Cupar. In 1950 he set up 'The Drapery House' at 135 South Street which he purchased for £7000 in 1950. He wrote of this in his book *Memoirs of a Provost*: 'The way was clear to alter the front and produce a display arcade. In the course of the next few years, two areas of the shop had the latest glass fittings at a cost of over £1000 each; one was by Heggie and Aitchieson of Edinburgh.' The shop offered a large selection of clothing, household linen, bales of material of all sorts and haberdashery items. Mr Fordyce retired in 1961, and the arcade and fine fittings were eventually swept away and the property split up.

The Fairfield Drapery was established at 68-72 Market Street in 1895 by Robert Thomson. There were branches of Fairfield Stores at Dunfermline, Kirkcaldy, Cupar and Buckhaven. The founder of the business was Peter Thomson who died in 1895; he was a draper and hatter of Kirkcaldy. The St Andrews shop advertised in 1907 as 'Dress and Mantle Makers' and in 1915, 'Drapery, Clothing, Boots, Shoes, Dress making, Millinery & Tailoring. SATISFACTION GUARANTEED'. It also ran a 'Servants Registry'. In 1950 the shop specialised in ladies and gentlemen's clothing and in dress materials. I recall clearly that on one counter there was always a large bowl of odd buttons which you stirred around until you sighted one similar to your missing one! When the smaller items of haberdashery came to be sold in packages it was irritating – you could no longer be thrifty and buy just the amount you wanted, such as a single button! And thrifty we were when we came in 1950, as we still had ration cards. For a time quite a lot of entertaining was done by inviting friends in to tea or to coffee in the evening. I remember helping Mrs Donald Mills to make the sandwiches for a meeting at her house. 'Just use the margarine,' she said 'and only on the bottom slice of bread.' I was surprised – at the farm I had made the butter in a churn.

There was a tailor in Argyle Street, Mr Edie, who actually worked sitting cross-legged on a bench at the window of his shop; his son succeeded him. Mr Burns had a tailor's business at 137 South Street, and another tailor had a shop at 7 College Street. There were several dressmakers in the town, and I suppose most households had a Singer sewing machine. My friend 'Buffer' Woodward used to have a dressmaker who came regularly for a period of days to make garments for herself, her husband Ferdy and their four daughters. Knitting wool and embroidery thread were in great demand. Greensmith Downes was a 'good' dress shop on the corner of Bell Street and Market Street. Nearby at Greyfriars Garden was Mr Sturrock, hairdresser. Mrs Taylor's dress shop and milliner at 125 South Street was elegant within and without. The façade remains, and the windows remind me of the story of a strong-minded elderly lady who lived in Hepburn Gardens. When she announced that she was changing her car for one of a new make, friends tried in vain to persuade her that she should give up driving. Central Motors rang up to say that the car had arrived, and she went down to collect it, insisting on driving away herself without any instruction. The car shot across South Street and landed in the windows of Mrs Taylor's shop; no one was hurt. A friend who was cycling past dismounted, went to the driver's window, said 'I told you so', and departed. The other important clothes shop was Caird's at 19 Bell Street, run by Sandy Caird who lived in Windmill Road. There were departments for ladies and for gentlemen, and an additional Caird's shop across the road sold hosiery, gloves etc. When they closed down 1986 it was hard to see how St Andrews could manage. On New Year's Day you met everyone you knew at the Caird's Sale. One year I was standing at the top of the stairs and heard a university lecturer address the crowd: 'Well, that's it', he said 'See you all at the party tonight.' 'What a wonderful friendly place this is', I thought happily.

The other great New Year's Day sale was at the Woollen Mill, set up by the Philip brothers, first sited in Church Street and then at The Links. Tots of whisky were handed out to the queue. Two tight-lipped ladies in front of me were whispering: 'Did you see Mrs --- taking whisky at ten thirty in the morning?' 'Yes, DIS-graceful.' The famous St Andrews Woollen Mill closed down three years ago.

Woolworths branch store in Market Street was set up in the early 1930s. Trees on the site had to be taken down, and this resulted in the removal of all the trees in Market Street. St Katharines and St Leonards girls were not allowed to go into the shops, in particular Woolworths, or to either of the cinemas 'in case of germs'. They were even forbidden to walk along Market Street! The branch of Boots which replaced Smith and Govans, chemists, at 109 South Street was a great asset to me, as they had a library upstairs. Having become a member, you left a notebook with a list of books and, each time you called, there was an item ready. The Town Library was small and was housed in Queens Gardens, and the Hay Fleming Reference Library was for a time at Kinburn House.

One ironmonger was (and remains the only one today) John Wilson at 169-171 South Street; the business established in 1894. It is one of the few shops in St Andrews with the old type of house windows. There was also McKenzie's at 113 South Street and A.M. Bridges (established 1830) at 72 South Street and 108 South Street. Mr Bridges was the father of Millie Bridges who married A.B. Paterson; their children, Caroline and Hugh, came along the Lade Braes daily to my school at South View. Some parents brought their children to school on bicycle seats. In 1950 the cycle shops I knew in my student days were still there and thriving.

There was a shop across from the Post Office owned by Stewart Marks who lived in Hepburn Gardens; he sold wireless sets and fishing tackle. He was quite a character and a great talker. One day I said to him, 'I must be off to look at the sea.' 'The sea ?', he said, 'What's that? I haven't seen it for about twenty years.' I wonder if he was joking? Perhaps not.

St Andrews

You can live here –
And never know the sea:
Broad streets run parallel,
The intersecting shoreward lanes,
Aimless, yield before they reach it –

Never slope down the harbour path
Where the women stretched the nets to mend
And the Long Pier screened the fishing fleet.

Never feel the sift of sand through toes,
Glancing across the estuary of Eden
Where Tentsmuir scrawls its dark tree line.

You can live here –
Circling and searching for the reward
Of a white-lined space to shuffle off your car
To stand half mesmerised
Before a chest of piled-up frozen fish –

Never look on castle walls
Tumbling seawards, held back
By the brace of the final towers.

Never walk the span between cathedral arches,
Picture the shrines of saints, the chances of gold,
Nor ever think you hear, between the winds, the vespers bell.

Mary Gatheral

Methven Simpson's Music Shop was at 3 Greyfriars Garden; the mosaic with the harp is still in the floor at the doorway. There was a good stock of pianos. I remember listening to gramophone records in one of the booths. In the 1930s Alexander Mason Nicholson started a business; he was a cycle and radio dealer. His son, Derek, joined the Bell Street business in 1962, and in 1969 took it over, dealing mainly with television and radio sales and repairs, and maintaining a very high standard of service. He is presently giving up the sales side and will work on repairs to electrical equipment.

Down at Golf Place and the Links there are two long established golf businesses known worldwide. Auchterlonie's was founded in 1894, and the Tom Morris business dates from 1864, but did not move to the present site overlooking the 18th green until 1884.

So which is the oldest shop still trading from its original site? John Macgregor was born in Market Street in September 1832. His father – also John Macgregor – and family emigrated in the summer of 1848. But young John decided to remain here and set up as a master painter in College Street. Shortly afterwards he moved to a shop in Market Street, next door to the house where he had been born. He moved again to a house at the top of College Street, and then his business expanded and flourished, and it occupied 69-73 Market Street. The firm had businesses as cabinetmakers, undertakers, upholsterers, painters, glaziers and paperhangers! In March 1857 he opened branches in Anstruther and Crail, and in November that year he took out a licence as an auctioneer and appraiser. He was elected a member of the Town Council in 1862, became Dean of Guild in 1867, Magistrate from 1868 to 1892, and then served as Provost from 1893 to 1899. There was a fine photograph (hanging in the present café until recently) of the Macgregor staff, tradesmen of various sorts in impressive array. John Macgregor died in April 1905. His son David took over the painting and decorating (later sold to J.C. Rolland), and his son

James the auctioneering and cabinet-making business. These two sons died in 1936 and 1938. The undertaking and the auctioneering businesses were then run by Mr Swankie, and it was he and his son who developed the large shop as we knew it in 1950. The furniture store was extensive: carpets, linoleums, rugs, bedding, dining room and drawing room suites, kitchen and bathroom fittings. At one time we heard that Macgregors had obtained a water bed which was on view and for sale. I should think half the town went to examine it and try it out. Word went round (possibly untrue) that unfortunately it had sprung a leak! The auction rooms were then at the far east end of Market Street (where Kidston Court is now), and the monthly auctions were an occasion. The addicts arrived early on the scene to occupy the front row of comfortable easy chairs. Mr Swankie conducted the proceedings. He used to cry, 'Hold it up, let them see it' to Mr Shelly, who was a tall well-built man. He would hoist the specimen (such as an armchair) aloft like the strong man at a circus. If there was a piano to be auctioned Mr Swankie would enliven the audience by playing some tunes on it.

Foster's had a good antique shop at 5-6 Bell Street. In 1890 James Pirie established a business as a china merchant at 131 South Street, and had moved to 7 Greyfriars Garden by 1935; the shop, which is still there, has become well known as a specialist in crystal and fine china. Near the West Port there was another china shop, Mercer's, started by John Mercer in 1898; the Misses Mercer who later served in it seemed to me to be very old.

The Victoria Café which I knew so well as a student still had the open-air trellised area on the Bell street side. A friend of mine remembers that each waitress at the Victoria Cafe wore a different coloured ribbon on her uniform and this matched ribbons on the tables which she served.

The Hotels

There were many well-established hotels operating in the fifties, but most were to close in the next decades. The old Crown Inn in Abbey Street was demolished for road widening in 1969. David Bryce's 1866 West Park Hotel in St Mary's Place was pulled down in 1976 to make way for the new Students' Union. The Royal Hotel (118 South Street) – probably by George Rae in 1857 and extended by Milne in 1894 – was taken over by the University in 1963, and as Southgait Hall was a staff club and residence, with student flats erected behind it. It is presently up for sale. St Regulus Hotel, 23 Queens Gardens, built in 1864-5 (George Rae?) became a university residence in 1960. The Grand Hotel of 1895 was designed by James Monro. The story of its origin which I heard was this: a certain businessman applied for membership of the Royal and Ancient; this was refused, whereupon he bought the site and promised his new hotel would make the R. and A. Clubhouse look pretty silly. It is indeed conspicuous in colour (the railway had made it possible to bring red sandstone from Dumfriesshire) and in size; it is six storeys high and had 130 bedrooms. In the late 1940s, there was a great outcry about an offer for the Hotel by the Catholic Church, for use as a Training Seminary for Roman Catholic priests. At a public meeting a professor from St Marys gave warnings that St Andrews might become 'a Roman Catholic centre for propaganda' – unthinkable, because of the part it had played in the Reformation. The owners of the Hotel accordingly turned down the offer, and it was subsequently bought by the University in 1949, and since then it has been the student residence Hamilton Hall. The dome to the north is now of fibreglass; it replaced the copper dome after a damaging fire caused by a workman's blowlamp. I watched the new dome being hoisted into place. Another university purchase was the Athol Hotel in Links Crescent, designed by John Milne in 1890 as a house called 'Alleynes'; this became the John Burnet Hall of Residence in 1967.

George Rae's 1851 Cross Keys Hotel at 85 Market Street was once a coaching inn. Today it retains the name and the bar, but has been converted into flats. The crossed keys sign – standing for food, drink and accommodation – is still there. In 1982 the same thing happened to The Star across the road. This was a flourishing concern when bought by William Rusack in 1875; there was a large yard with stables at the rear. The Rusacks sold it in 1886. Jesse Hall's Station and Windsor Hotel (1870) at 3-6 Alexandra Place – subsequently renamed the Alexandra – was sold, and in the late 1960s was changed for various uses. The Imperial Temperance Hotel in North Street (David Henry, 1881) remains as the Argyl Hotel. It is no longer 'Temperance'. Men of the Polish army were billeted there during the War, and it had the distinction of having a ballroom added in 1920.

The Golf Hotel had a fine situation, on the corner of Golf Place and The Links. It was built in 1879 for Mr David Robertson on the site of the villa owned by Allan Robertson's family, and was very popular with golfers. The hotel changed hands twice: first to the Honeymans and then to the Bruces. The business went into liquidation about 1976. It was bought by a Glasgow firm who turned the corner part into flats. The basement and another area were bought by the Philip Brothers of the Woollen Mill, who also acquired the previous workshops of Forgan, golf club manufacturers which had been closed down in 1963. The Woollen Mill was the haunt of tourists and seems to have been famous over half the world! For the last three years, since the Philips retired from business and the R. and A. bought the premises, bewildered visitors to the town gaze at the giant cranes and the polythene-shrouded skeleton and ask passers-by, 'Can you tell me, is this the woollen mill?'

Near the Golf Hotel there was The Links on the south-east corner of Golf Place. I am told that it was there in 1804, and also that when the first Open Golf Championship took place in St Andrews the Register was kept at the Links Hotel. For a time about 1900 it was known as the Bicycle Inn. Whenever there are golfing events in St Andrews, its customers flood out on to the pavement.

There are other smaller – but excellent – hotels which were here in the mid twentieth century. Boarding houses in the Murray Park and Murray Place continue to thrive. On the Scores, both the Russell Hotel and the St Andrews Golf Hotel were set up in premises which had previously been private houses.

Only two of the large old hotels are still in business. One is The Scores Hotel, opened *c.* 1931; the main part (attributed to John Milne, 1880) was once St Salvator's School. The other is Rusacks Marine Hotel. Ronnie Rusack, the grandson of William Rusack, is writing the story of this well-known family. The founder of the hotel was Johann Kristoff Wilhelm Rusack. The family originated from Poland, but he was born in Bad Harzburg twenty-five years after the birth of his brother who became manager of a large hotel in Hamburg. For a time Wilhelm worked at this hotel, and then emigrated to Scotland, gaining further experience at the Queen Street Hotel, Glasgow, and known as William Rusack. There he met Janet McIntyre, who often stayed at this hotel, and after they married they went to the Station Hotel, Perth. Janet visited St Andrews and thought it would be a good place in which to bring up their family. Eventually they were able to buy the reputable Star Hotel which became even more prestigious. The family increased – there were to be eight children. The Rusacks set up a new private hotel in the more peaceful Abbotsford Place (at the west end of the terrace). In 1885 William's application for British citizenship was approved. Janet (Mrs Rusack) negotiated the purchase of a piece of land on the Links. It had been used as a drying green and for the parking of a lifeboat. And here the grand five-storey Rusacks Marine Hotel was built, and The Star and The Abbotsford were sold. The new hotel opened in March 1887, the great year of Queen Victoria's Golden Jubilee. There was a fine winter garden (where the car park is now), private suites, and electric lift and excellent service by German waiters. It became the place where the wealthy and the famous stayed. Extensions were made in 1892 and 1894. Janet's acumen led to the purchase of Bogward Farm which provided milk and produce for the hotel. It was managed by Harry, the oldest son, when he grew up.

The third son. Louis, was killed in the battle of the Somme. The second son, David, who was wounded at Gallipoli, took over the Hotel when his father died in 1916. It was a golden time: Edward Prince of Wales came to stay and he and David became friends. The Rothschilds, the Vanderbilts and of course many of the famous golfers stayed at The Rusack Marine. Captain David Rusack was well known in St Andrews; he was founder of the British Legion and became chairman of the St Andrews Branch, and was associated with the Boy Scouts. The hotel was taken over by the Army during the 1939 war, and David and his wife lived at their house, Fairways, until they emigrated to Durban in 1949.

The hotel was renovated and put in the hands of a manager; the acumen of the Rusacks was missed, and it eventually went into liquidation. It was bought by Will Fyffe, the comedian, but there was a tragedy when he fell from a window of the hotel and was killed. It was purchased by the Aberdeen Hotel Company and has sailed through the years. It is now owned by Macdonald Hotels. A further twenty bedrooms have been added – a visible sign of its good health.

The fact that so many well-known hotels closed in the second half of the century may be due to a number of reasons; the main one was surely the huge increase in people taking holidays abroad. Did the loss of our railway line have an effect? When Beeching was making his rail cuts and the line was obviously at risk, the Town Council gave planning permission for the erection of 'The British Transport Hotel' on a rather messy site where the first railway station had been and where there were a goods yard and coal storage huts. As a railway hotel, surely the link must be retained? But apart from that, a sound reason for granting planning permission was the estimate that it would bring in £25,000 in rates. Conditions were made that the outline of the old coal sheds had to be retained as markers for the line the golfers should take when driving to the seventeenth green. There is a photograph in T.T. Fordyce's book of himself, Mr Stewart (Assistant General Manager of British Railways) and Mr Frank viewing a model of the hotel; it looks like a liner in dock. At the opening on 25 June 1968 Provost Fordyce said, 'We all share a delight that we are each in our own way associated with the birth of this beautiful hotel. … we hope it may grow in grace and favour.' The size and the starkness of the building on this exposed and vulnerable site made it seem, to many, a violation of the landscape. A.B. Paterson's comment was 'a concrete fortress'. It was bought by Mr Frank Sheridan in 1984 and the name was changed to 'The Old Course Hotel and Country Club'. A few years later a consortium of businessmen bought it, and it was renamed 'The Old Course Hotel'. Whether the succession of attempts to mitigate its ugliness has helped or not is a matter of opinion. To me it looks like an enlargement of a construction which children made with giant Lego blocks. But as the Old Course Hotel, it is prestigious and valuable at times of golfing events. The irony (or do I mean treachery?) was that its opening to the public coincided with the removal of the railway lines between Leuchars and St Andrews.

We used that St Andrews line on our frequent journeys south at holidays. Another time we went from St Andrews to Perth and on to Kingussie to stay with the Milligans at their holiday house there. We also went to Glasgow from St Andrews station, and I recall our first such journey on a hot summer's day. The windows of our carriage were wide open. The embankments were thick with wild flowers; given extraordinarily long arms, one could have leant out and picked a bunch. The run round the East Neuk towns was a joy, made even more exciting by a young man who played his violin!

General Smuts (second from right) was installed as Rector of St Andrews University in 1934. He is seen with, from left, Principal Sir James Irvine, Mr Stanley Baldwin, Chancellor, and Sir J.M. Barrie, Chancellor of Edinburgh University and former Rector.

A photograph of the harbour taken by George Washington Westwood, c 1890

Westerlee, Kennedy Gardens, 1865-68

College Church c 1878

Rathmore, Kennedy Gardens, 1861

'Joan's House', 18th Century., South Castle Street, saved from demolition by the Preservation Trust

The Edwardian Building which housed grocers Aikman and Terras

South Court, south face, c. 1666

The Preservation Trust Museum, North Street, early 18th c.

St Andrews and the War

I think that when I came back to St Andrews in 1950 there was not much talk of the war, and there was little physical trace. St Andrews had two incidents when bombs fell; the first was in October 1940 when a string of bombs was jettisoned. One wrecked a house in Greenside Place, but the lady who lived there was out. The second fell in Westburn Lane and damaged the Geology Department; the third landed in St Mary's quad and scattered 14,000 books from the library. In 1944 bombs fell in Nelson Street and Bowling Green Road, and twelve people were killed. Other visible reminders of the war were the concrete anti-tank defences on the beaches erected by the Polish army. Those at Tentsmuir very gradually gave way to the poundings of the waves, and the sand has buried the remains. Remnants of the St Andrews' barriers are still to be seen near the Eden.

In Alwyn Clark's book *The McKenzie Sisters*, we learn of the art classes (drawing and engraving) which the artists Winifred McKenzie and Annabel Kidston ran for the Polish and British troops stationed locally. The classes were held in a spare room in Upper College Hall which was then the home of the Psychology Department. Exhibitions of their work were held in Lower College Hall, and in May 1943 a splendid exhibition was mounted in Edinburgh at the National Gallery of Scotland of the works of twenty-eight Polish and seventeen British soldiers. Three specially gifted Poles were asked by the Commanding Officer to produce ideas for a memorial to commemorate the Polish role as defenders of this coast when it was threatened. The fine mosaic which they designed and executed is on the outside of the Town Hall in Queens Gardens. Much later a bronze portrait of General Sikorski was set up in Kinburn Park. Some of the Polish soldiers settled in St Andrews after the war and played an important part of the life of the community. They established a St Andrews Polish Club which still continues.

I found that in St Andrews in the fifties entertaining often took the form of an invitation to 'coffee after your evening meal'. Most of the houses did not have central heating, and in winter one wore layers of clothes; unless you were seated close to the fire it was cold. Somebody said, 'A lot of club members [St Rule's] have two good thick suits, one for day wear and the other to change into for the evening.' In 1940 my friend Nandy Johnston came as a young bride to Rathelpie, the Martyrs Manse in Kennedy Gardens, a beautiful spacious house with a large garden. The warmest room in the house was the bathroom where the hot water tank presided. The drawing room had a lovely view and on clear days they could see Schiehallion. There was an anthracite stove in the dining room, and in the kitchen there was a coal stove and a gas cooker, but no water. The scullery faced north and had a sink and stone shelves. The laundry room had a huge boiler on top of a coal-burning fire, laundry tubs and a large wringer. A stair from this room led to the maids' bedrooms – but unfortunately there were no maids! I visited the Johnstons in 1947 and saw some golf, but soon after that they emigrated to Canada.

Under Sir James Irvine the University had continued to grow steadily. He was fulfilling his objectives to create an entirely residential university, a centre of excellence, the numbers balanced with the size of St Andrews, and to maintain good relationships between Town and Gown. But the happy years were coming to an end. Lady Irvine writes of the situation just before the war.

> Still deepening war-clouds darkened our horizon and against this background of world-wide unease, Jim faced troubles within the university for the first time in sixteen years of office.
>
> I shall write as little as may be about this controversy but find it impossible to pass over, without comment, matters which made an irreparable mark on Jim and which shadowed his last years. … The Dundee controversy emerged insignificantly enough in a series of

> articles published in the local press of Dundee, which attacked the University policy in general and Jim's administration of the affiliated college in Dundee in particular. The articles were ill-informed, their statements inaccurate, and their figures incorrect, so it followed that their implications were far from the truth. ... University College, itself the bone of the contention, remained silent and dignified. In St Andrews there was a sympathetic conspiracy of silence among the members of the Senate. ...[Jim's] creed was simple, unshakeable and abundantly clear to all who understood university affairs. He believed that the ancient foundation in St Andrews was the fountainhead of the University: that the colleges had their own status and importance for they were the eyes, hands, and feet of the body corporate: each college had its own necessary contribution to make. To him it was as clear, as inevitable as that. 'The Part cannot be greater than the whole' he declared, 'and that is the vain ambition of the city of Dundee'.
>
> Jim's policy for the development of the college in Dundee never swerved; it was the furtherance of those subjects which must have a busy and prosperous city for their background – Engineering and its allied sciences, Law and Education. The School of Medicine was also in this category and was already flourishing and successful. He was determined to avoid the duplication of chairs in Arts subjects, and by this means to strengthen the integration of University College students with their alma mater by taking the honours year in St Andrews.

Principal Donaldson (1890-1915) had not liked the terms of the affiliation, on the grounds that he felt it would be unworkable. University College Dundee was not incorporated in the same way as the other two colleges: it retained what Dr Cant described as 'substantial independence while acquiring a formidable interest in the control of the university'. From 1946 General Douglas Wimberley was the new full-time Principal of University College; he felt the Court was not sympathetic to Dundee. There were demands that the Medical School, the dental schools and the students of education should all come under University College. There was talk of Dundee becoming a university. Approaches were made to the Secretary of State, and in 1949 Lord Cooper's scheme for closer integration failed to get the support of the University. A Royal Commission under Lord Tedder sat and put forward a radical, complex reorganisation to be effected by legislation. Principal Irvine recommended its adoption to the University Court in 1952.

After gaining his BSc Hons at St Andrews Nigel, the son of Sir James and Lady Irvine, had gone up to Oxford to study Law. When war broke out he had already received his commission in the RNVR and was away for his training. Later he took a course in radar, and was on the Murmansk convoy in the Arctic. Lady Irvine and Veronica turned to Red Cross work (Deanscourt was the centre), and Lady Irvine stuck to the work for the five years of war. Veronica was married to Richard Gandy, and in 1941 Sir James and Lady Irvine's first grandchild was born in Edinburgh. Felicity drove a large bus carrying cadets between St Andrews and Leuchars aerodrome.

Lady Irvine writes of University House: 'Eventually we were left with no one in the house but an elderly gardener who carried coal for me and kept the old-fashioned range stoked and burning clearly.' The historian Miss Caroline Ketelbey had bought and restored two old stone cottages at South Flisk, near Blebo Craigs. She sold this property to the Principal in 1942 – it was to be a present to his wife. Here the Irvine family had a peaceful refuge. Nigel was there briefly before going to join his ship 'The Nigeria' in Charleston, Carolina. Nigel wrote of Flisk, 'I would rather have one stony acre in Fife than a beautiful estate in any country in Britain.' But from Lady Irvine's description Flisk had its own beauty. Nigel's wedding to Cecilia Banister took place in London in December 1943. Lady Irvine had gone ahead to London, but was called back to St Andrews as Sir James had taken ill. They both missed this important event. Nigel had to rejoin his ship – now at Chatham – the day after the wedding, and in January the ship sailed east.

In the spring of 1944 Sir James was (with his characteristic determination) recovering from an illness brought on by overwork. For some time before the war Sir Oliver Stanley, who was Secretary of State for the Commonwealth, saw that it was necessary, as a preliminary to the Commonwealth countries achieving autonomy, to improve the facilities for higher education in the more isolated and backward regions. A commission was set up under Mr Justice Asquith, and Sir James Irvine was one of its members. His wife writes, 'While still in the hands of a hospital nurse, and before he had been out of bed, Jim had yielded to the persuasions of Mr Oliver Stanley to undertake this work in the West Indies. So Sir James, as Chairman of the committee of seven members, left London on 17 February for a devious wartime journey to Trinidad. The initial work, which took five months, involved visits to British Guiana, Puerto Rico, Jamaica and Trinidad, then to Washington and Montreal. The party was due back in England on 5 June.

On 2 June, after her work at Deanscourt, Lady Irvine took the bus to Flisk where she and Felicity were staying. Felicity was late home. When she arrived she had to break the news that Nigel had been accidentally drowned while in Ceylon on sick leave from his ship after a bad bout of tropical fever. His name is on the St Andrews war memorial along with those of another hundred St Andrews men who lost their lives. (When he lived in St Andrews, Nigel had constructed a sand yacht which brought sand yachting to the West Sands. This sport continued, and at Easter 1972 the British Sand Yacht titles races were held there.)

The committee's report was completed in July after the members had come home; the work continued. Sir James returned to Jamaica in 1947 and 1948; in an article in the *Alumnus Chronicle* in 1949 the Principal wrote:

> For the past five years I have seen this great educational experiment in the West Indies at work. The four trips I have made to the Colonies have been to me an inspiration and it is a rich reward to see once again my dreams come true and a second university taking shape as foreseen in vision. ...
>
> It is more than the governmental machinery of St Andrews that has been transplanted to the West Indies, for the spirit of St Andrews has already captured the imagination of students and staff. Our name is honoured by our distant fellow-citizens; the scarlet gown in lighter weight ... has been adopted as the undergraduate dress, and ceremonies will be in line with traditional usage.

In 1949, accompanied by his wife and daughter Felicity, Sir James returned to Jamaica to lay the foundation stone of the first Hall of Residence which was called by his name. On 20 September 1950 the 500th anniversary of St Salvator's College was celebrated in St Andrews in the presence of Her Majesty the Queen.

In the early summer of 1951 Sir James Irvine suffered a severe coronary thrombosis and was in hospital for nine weeks. He returned to convalesce at Flisk, and in the autumn he resumed work. He died after a night's illness on the morning of 12 June 1952. His daughter Veronica wrote, 'His last day had been happy and like many others – a meeting in the afternoon and then tea in the garden. For fifty-seven years he had served the University faithfully and well. He had never had to lay down his tools, never had to leave St Andrews.'

I have often thought of all he achieved for the University and for the town in his time here. Ronald Cant describes him as a liberal autocrat who had the good of the University at heart. He was a dedicated man, a man of vision. When I saw his tombstone in the East Cemetery, near the gates on to the Pends, I thought of him in his prime, a leader who scarcely stopped to consider himself. He was a handsome man, not tall but of great stature, and an inspiring speaker. Sir Hector Hetherington gave the funeral oration at the service in St Salvator's Chapel. He said, 'To him, more than any other, the University owes the remarkable enlargement of its academic resources, and the seemly beauty of its material estate. He loved St Andrews with all the strength of an eager and generous heart, and gave to it the full service of all his powers.'

Chapter 5

THE ST ANDREWS PRESERVATION TRUST

The previous chapters have given impressions of life in St Andrews in the first fifty years of the twentieth century. We now need to go back in time to the formation of the St Andrews Preservation Trust and its history up to date. To do this, we use a different format. This tells the story of what Lady Irvine called 'This place of struggle and change, progress and loss'. The main sources of information are the *Trust's Annual Report and Year Book 1938-2000* and a handbook, *Conservation in St Andrews*, published by the Trust in 1963.

In 1931 a meeting took place of representatives of the University Court and of the St Andrews Town Council, and they appointed a committee to co-operate in their joint interests. These stemmed from the concern felt by a group of St Andrews citizens, among them Principal Sir James Irvine, Mr Norman Boase, Miss Annabel Kidston, and Mr R.G. Cant, about a state shared with other historic cities and towns: 'St Andrews had been changing and developing to an extent undreamed of by previous generations, and there was anxiety lest in a short time the whole traditional character of the city might be, if not destroyed, irreparably damaged'. The Provost was Mr Norman Boase who was a staunch supporter of the scheme, but retired from office in October 1937 and died the following March.

As the years went by and certain important houses were lost or under threat, it seemed necessary to involve the public. In June 1937 an exhibition was held in St Andrews at the Convention of the Royal Incorporation of Architects of Scotland. This exhibition was arranged by Miss Annabel Kidston and was of a collection of photographs of old houses taken by two members of the University staff, Dr J.Y. Macdonald and Dr David Jack; the choice of sites for these photos was from a list drawn up by Mr R.G. Cant and Mr A.B. Paterson (the well-known St Andrews journalist). This proved a good way of arousing public interest and stressing the urgency of the matter. In July 1937 a meeting was called by the Principal of St Mary's, the Very Reverend Harry Miller, and on the initiation of Miss Kidston it was decided to form an organisation 'to preserve old houses and more generally the entire character of St Andrews'. In the Autumn there was a second showing of the exhibition, to which were added water-colour paintings by Miss Ada Walker. As many as 1100 people signed a book to show their support for the formation of the proposed society.

As a result the St Andrews Preservation Trust was founded at a public meeting held on 1 December 1937. The Very Reverend Harry Miller was in the chair. Sir James Irvine and Professor Baxter addressed the Meeting. Provost Reid proposed the motion for the formation of a St Andrews Preservation Trust, and it was carried. By March 1938 the Trust was recognised as a public body. The *ex-officio* members were to be the Principal of the University, the Provost of St Andrews, and the Convener of the County Council. A committee was elected – the Honorary President: the Very Rev. J. Harry Miller; Honorary Vice Presidents: the Earl of Elgin and Sir James Irvine; Trustees: Mr David Russell of Silverburn, Mr R. G. Cant, Provost John Reid, Professor D'Arcy Thomson, Dr James Younger, Miss Kidston, Miss Low, Miss C. Moir, Mr Alexander Gilchrist (Secretary). Two sub-committees were formed: 1. Finance; 2. Archaeological and artistic under Mr Ronald Cant. By 31 December 1937 there were 351 members of which 81 were life members.

Property

Louden's Close

This close consisted of 146-148, facing on to South Street, the entry and the houses in the Close; 146-148 and two of the Close houses probably belong to the early eighteenth century, and two others to the late eighteenth century. In 1939 the whole property was purchased from the Louden family with the aid of a special grant from the Pilgrim Trust; this Trust, and also the Dalrymple Archaeological Fund, later gave a grant for the renovation works.

In order to make accommodation for the St Andrews Girls' Club (to be named the Torch Club), the plan of the Trustees was to turn the house with the South Street frontage into a four-roomed apartment which would be sold. The downstairs part, where the ceilings were too low for a dwelling, would make a Hall for the Torch Club, and the adjacent houses (numbers 1 and 2 in the Close) would provide clubrooms. The later Close houses would eventually be repaired and put up for sale. These plans took a long time to implement, partly because of the outbreak of war, and ensuing delays in getting permits, finding workmen and obtaining materials.

Work on the ground floor of 146-148 and the two adjoining Close houses was completed by January 1941, the total cost being £1100, but for another two years the frontage house stood at one storey. Eventually the separate apartment and the Close houses were completed (although one had to be demolished). The property was put up for roup and fetched the sum of £3650. This big project, carried out successfully but taking dauntingly long, was one of several others to follow.

166-168 South Street

A second property, also belonging to Mr Louden was a house near Louden's Close, the only remaining house in South Street with an outside stair; it and the building behind it were under a threat of demolition. The Trust bought this house but had to defer a decision on it. The Trustees eventually decided that, because of its poor condition, they could not undertake the renovation; it was put up for sale but remained unsold. In November 1952 the house collapsed under a heavy rain-storm. There was a most encouraging conclusion to this saga. In June 1954 Miss Low of South Street (formerly of Blebo House) offered to pay for the reconstruction of the property. The plans were approved and the work went ahead. It was sold for £5,330, and Miss Low donated the whole amount to the Trust for its future work.

11 South Castle Street

To go back in time to 1938, 11 South Castle Street was under a demolition order as 'unfit for human habitation' *(I am struck by how familiar that phrase was before and after the war, and how far away that seems now!).* This small property dating from about 1700 was later known as 'Joan's House'– Joan being one of the old fisherfolk who lived in that part of St Andrews. (St Gregory's nearby was built in 1921 as flatted housing for fishermen.) Joan's House was bought by the Trust on 15 February 1938. In view of the impending road changes which might involve its demolition, the Trust rented it as a store. In 1964 when the plan was amended, the Trustees decided to bring it back into use as a house. It was sold to a buyer who would reconstruct it, and was finally restored and occupied in 1966. *(Now, in the twenty-first century, it stands as a reminder of the distant past, with pots of flowers on the outside stair. If you look up you will see a terra-cotta cat and mouse on the pantiles!)* And, amazingly, an excellent photograph of Joan herself is hung in the Trust Museum.

Baker Lane

In 1940 there was a Public Inquiry with regard to a bid by the St Andrews Town Council to retain its planning powers. In this it was successful, partly due to the fact that a Preservation Trust had been formed, was working with the Council and backed the appeal. During the next two or more decades co-operation between the Trust and the Town Council was close, and usefully effective. Plans had been drawn up by the Council for the renovation of Baker Lane, shown to the Trust, and had its support. However, the Department of Health did not concur, and it was necessary to agree to pull down the houses on the west side of the Lane. *(I must have walked along there hundreds of times – the small area of gardens lifts the heart. Only by the chimney end to the south are there traces of the houses. In that wall is a carving of a head; Ronald Cant once said to me he thought it was the top of the old Mercat Cross.)*

Changes in Trust Strategy

The Trust quickly gained momentum and membership increased, but was to fall again during the War. The Trust was never intended merely as an Amenity Body. It was a public non-profit-making company founded to work in the public interest. In its long history it has always had a role as watchdog, examining all planning applications regarding property, and taking relevant action, but it has also been greatly concerned with larger issues. In 1939 there was a change in strategy; a resolution was passed giving a wider scope of power to members of the Association to take over property which was not necessarily deemed of archaeological or artistic worth. In some cases where property belonged to the Trust, it might be transferred to some other body such as the local authority, to be held and maintained. The aim of the Trust was not to acquire property, but to prevent its destruction and secure its preservation.

The War Years

The Trust continued to do valuable work throughout the war years. After the death of Mr Norman Boase in 1938, his brother Mr Philip Boase became a trustee and was later Chairman. In the report of 1941, Mr Cant the Chairman wrote: 'Even when hemmed in by the grim necessities of the present, hard though it may be, we must not forget either the future or the past of our nation, our countryside or our cities.' The Town Council held a list of property carefully compiled by the Trust – the work of Mr Cant and based mainly on a National Trust memorandum. Another valuable piece of work, with Miss Kidston as convener, was to make duplicates of photographs already taken. Further photos and drawings were added to this collection. By 1942 these records were complete; they were catalogued and put on microfilm.

In 1943 the Trust submitted to the Town Council an additional list of buildings which were of worth, to be included in the original draft scheme of buildings. This was considered by the Council, which all along was co-operative.

Recommendations by the Trust

In 1944 the Trust handed to the Town Council a document of recommendations with regard to Town Planning. In view of what has happened in the next sixty years, and especially what is happening today, these are very interesting and show great foresight. This is the list:

1. All existing buildings on the Town Council's list should be protected by scheduling in terms of the earlier suggestions of the Trust.
2. There should be controls established over the siting and design

of new buildings in the historic part of the city to ensure they conform to the character of older adjacent buildings and of the city in general.

3. Outside the old city all new developments should be carefully controlled so as to preserve the characteristic aspect of St Andrews. In the case of the Municipal Housing schemes, the Town Council might take advantage of the provisions of the Housing (Scotland) Act (1935) to appoint a local advisory committee to represent archaeological and other artistic interests.
4. Plans should be made for the preservation of mature trees.
5. There should be a measure of control over the shop frontages, street furniture, etc., and advertisements.
6. To preserve the view of the old city and also to maintain access, and for it to be protected on all sides, green belts should be considered and developed, running outwards from the city centre.
7. To ensure the full preservation of the amenities of the city and the safety of buildings in the older streets, particular attention should be given to the question of heavy traffic in relation to the historic centre.
8. Consideration should be given to such matters as the restoration of certain street names, restoration of the Mercat Cross (sadly never accomplished), and the provision of a local History Museum. South Court was suggested as a possible venue.

During the War the numbers of members fell slightly; by 1947 the membership was 615, of which 170 were life members.

The New Main Route, 1944-50

In October 1944 the Trust considered plans brought out by the Town Council Planning Consultant. These featured a development of the existing road plan along North Street, to use South Castle Street, Abbey Street and Abbey Walk. This was a tentative plan and had to be submitted to the Department of Health; it was important in that it might form part of the projected trunk route for the East of Fife. The Trust objected to the plan on these grounds: because the width of a trunk road by statute must be sixty feet which would entail the demolition of houses in South Castle Street (including 'Joan's House'). Mr Philip Boase proposed that the Trust should have a survey made regarding a possible road to by-pass the town; this was agreed. The route recommended by Mr Reid of Masson, Blyth and Blyth was: after entering by Petherum Bridge, up City Brae, and (with the West Port on the left) down Melbourne Brae and out to the south, thus avoiding the Town Centre. They pointed out that all recent official announcements had stressed that trunk roads should by-pass villages and towns.

The question of road widening was of interest to the Citizens Advisory Council which had been formed at the instigation of Sir James Irvine, and included representatives from the University, St Leonards School, the Merchants' Association, the Ratepayers' Society, the Co-operative Society and the Women Citizens and St Andrews Preservation Trust. The Trust sent representations to the Town Council, the County Council and the Ministry of War Transport regarding the Council's main road plan. The main objection made to the plan was 'to cut a real gash through South Castle St and Abbey Street would mean the loss of houses, of Dauphin Hill in particular, and of many mature trees'.

At this time, Miss Kidston and Mr Cant took part in a radio programme, a discussion about the renovation of old properties: the Trust's viewpoint was supported by a third (and entirely spontaneous) speaker, a Mr John Black who lived in South Castle Street; he had renovated his house and declared he was very happy and contented there.

The Trunk Road A918

The Trunk Road Bill was published on 24 January 1946 and became law in May. The route proposed from Guardbridge through St Andrews was to be along North Street to the Cathedral precinct, past the Roundel and down Abbey Street. The Town Council did not object, but the Trust objected on the following grounds:

1. Should heavy traffic develop from the south through increased industry, St Andrews ought to be by-passed. (*Note: it is now 2002; there is no bypass. The Roundel was repaired about twenty years ago; the repairs needed from the effects of heavy traffic on it were estimated at one million pounds. The work is now in progress.*)
2. Between the Roundel and the Pends the road was 26 feet wide with a right angle bend. There was concern whether this might involve road widening affecting the Roundel or the Pends.

The Preservation Trust and the Citizens Advisory Council protested. A meeting was convened by the County Council for representatives to meet Mr Burnett of the Ministry of War Transport, to discuss the proposed trunk road. Sir James Irvine spoke for the Trust and the Citizens Advisory Council. He reminded them of the unique character of St Andrews 'the only university city still standing amidst its old world settings and with all its historic famous buildings – the only town of its kind and date remaining in Scotland. It belongs not only to us but to the Nation.' Mr Burnett did not agree with the contentions; he had always regarded St Andrews as a terminus. He contended that most of the traffic was going to or from St Andrews. He assured them there would be no need to widen the road at the Roundel; he would consider 'sterilising of the route' in this part.

The next year (1950) the Trust sent a letter to the Town Council asking if the proposed road widths of sixty feet could be reduced. The Council compromised at fifty feet. The plan involved the demolition of a large house in South Street at the corner of Castle Street, and of Dauphin Hill (a very attractive late eighteenth century house on the corner of Abbey Walk and Greenside Place) and the loss of many good trees.

Property, up to 1949

The Trust was having a considerable effect; as it had recommended, several owners had restored property for their own use. At Balfour Place James Scott had succeeded in saving a row of picturesque red-roofed houses from demolition; two others were made into a dwelling house for Colonel and Mrs Hawes, both of whom were Trust members. (The Gifford family bought the house after Mrs Hawes' death.) The completion of the Balfour Place property brought the number of houses that were saved and restored by their purchasers under Trust guidelines to fourteen, in spite of the post-war difficulties over the shortage of building materials.

The Harbour and the Pier; the Gasworks

In 1948 the Trust gave £15 towards the repair of the pier. In December there was trouble at the harbour; a huge hole twelve yards long was torn in it by stormy seas. The Provost turned out everyone available, and they repaired the damage in fourteen days. Again there was damage by storms to the long pier in 1958 when the Trust donated £112 to a new Harbour Maintenance Fund. (At the time of writing, in 2002, the pier has been closed to the public for a year due to being unsafe. Money is being raised to repair it.)

In 1960 it was announced that the local gas supply was being linked to the central Scottish gas grid. The Trust asked the Town Council to plan a suitable lay-out. And it is there to see today, one of the most pleasing changes; the ugly gasworks which lay against the Cathedral precinct wall were cleared away, and grassy slopes laid to set off the medieval wall.

Property, 1950-51

A house at the back of 136 South Street in Imrie's Close, built in 1720, was, from 1749 to1774, the first Meeting Place of the St Andrews Secession Church (later the Hope Park Congregation). The house was condemned in 1937 and its owner, Mrs Bennett, became concerned about its future. A plaque placed on the outside wall reads:

1749. THE BURGHER KIRK. 1774
BEQUEATHED TO ST ANDREWS
PRESERVATION TRUST 1950
BY MRS JESSIE BENNETT

The Trust made plans for its preservation as a dwelling place for a single person and, with a grant from the Dalrymple Trust, it was renovated and furnished by Trust members Miss Aitken and Mrs Skinner. The house was then let.

On the initiative of Sir James Irvine the Chapel of St Leonards was at last being restored by the University with a grant from the Pilgrim Trust. The University was repairing two old houses at the north end of College Street.

In the sill of a window at 205 South Street a stone was found with an effigy of Bishop Wardlaw carved on it – it was thought to be part of the recumbent effigy on the lid of his tomb.

The University Physics Building, 1950-58

In 1950 the Town Council appointed Mr Maurice Taylor as Planning Officer for St Andrews and Dr Thomas Sharp as Planning Adviser. They played a big part in the stormy years of the next decade.

In May 1950 the University put out plans for a Physics building to be erected on the west side of Union Street. The height would be 40 to 50 feet. The Trust expressed anxiety about the design in this setting. It would entail demolishing several houses. Sir James Irvine addressed the Trust on this matter. He explained that the University was in urgent need of expansion for science, and there was no other central site. At first the Trust opposed the plan. The Town Council turned down the above plan, stating 'a large modern building of this size should not be erected in the main streets of the town'. The Council offered an alternative scheme, drawn up by Mr Sharp and published in the papers. This was on a site between West Burn Lane and Abbey Street; it would entail the loss of several small houses and large parts of the gardens of the South Street houses west of the lane. This would give the University a space for other necessary developments in the future. Compulsory purchasing powers would be used if necessary.

There was a special meeting of the Trust to consider an amended Union Street plan. Dr J.F. Allen and Dr Jack had worked out suggestions to make the building plan sympathetic. Four stories were essential, but ceiling heights had been reduced. Reluctantly the Trust voted in favour of the amended plan provided the Union street frontage was improved. The Chairman (Miss Kidston) had sent notice, *in absentia*, of her dissent.

The Town Council considered Mr Sharp's West Burn Lane scheme and turned it down on a majority vote, on the grounds that the University did not immediately need this land and that the use of compulsory purchase was objectionable. The University preferred the Union Street plan; the West Burn Lane plan would involve delay.

In 1952 the Town Council's Draft Development Plan proposals were considered. One proposal was to enlarge the 'green belt' areas such as the Lade Braes. Mr Somers' 1944 plan for the main road via South Castle Street was included in this draft plan; the intention was to create a green space. The Trust protested.

The Death of Sir James Irvine

Sir James died on the 12 June 1952. His life as Principal was so full that he was often under stress. His work had a tremendous effect on the growth of the University and on the development of the town. Not only was he one of the founders of the Preservation Trust, but he also accomplished a great deal for it. Quoting from Trust Reports 'he was ready at every stage to give advice and guidelines from his wide experience'. Sir James was Honorary President of the Trust from 1937 to the time of his death. (*I believe that his love of St Andrews shines out in the visible effects of his work. We should be thankful for all he achieved at a critical time.*) And what a team the Trust had! During those years Mr Alexander Gilchrist served continuously as Secretary and did not retire from this arduous voluntary post until 1966. From 1937 until the death of Sir James in 1952 there were four Chairmen: Miss Frances Warrack J.P. (1938-39), Mr R. G. Cant (1940-44), Mr Philip Boase (1945-48), Miss Annabel Kidston (1949-51). The list of Honorary Vice-Presidents is long and contains the names of eminent men, probably because of Sir James Irvine's work for the Trust. On his death his place as Honorary President was filled by the Earl of Crawford and Balcarres. It is the story of a group of loyal public-spirited people. Sir James died just before a run of very difficult years for the Town and the University. He was succeeded by Sir Malcom Knox, who was an *ex-officio* member of the Trust.

Local Inquiry into the Town Council's Development Plan

This began on 29 July 1955. Mr E. J. Keith Q.C. presided as commissioner. The case of the Preservation Trust was presented by Dr Coulthard, past Chairman of the Trust. The main objections were: (1) the realignment of Abbey Street, involving all the houses on the east side and Dauphin Hill on the west; (2) the extensive demolition of houses in South Castle Street; (3) the widening of South Castle Street might lead to the adoption of this road for the trunk road; (4) from the plans, the entry to South Street would be at an ungainly angle, making a gap wider than South Street itself; (5) the plan showed no awareness of the archaeological importance and historic charm of the city.

The result of the inquiry was very disappointing for the Trust. The Secretary of State approved the plans for Abbey Street and South Castle Street.

Continuation of the Physics Building Dispute, 1956

In January 1956 the Secretary of State gave general approval to the Development Plan for the Burgh, but stated that he was of the opinion that further consideration should be given to the question of allocating land, under the plan, to meet the future requirements of the University. In order that the matter might fully be considered, the Secretary of State issued a direction to the Town Council to submit proposals to him for the alterations of their plans, so as to allocate to the University an area of land adequate to the foreseeable building requirements and in the central part of the Burgh in reasonable proximity to its existing buildings. (*Comment: one appreciates the difficulties which the Council faced.*) Subsequently, but some time later, the Town Council withdrew the plan for widening South Castle Street.

In March the University architects, Holford and Partners, recommended that the University should ask the Town Council for a survey of the land bounded by South Street, Abbey Street, Queens Terrace, Greenside Place, Kinnessburn and Lade Braes Lane to see if a large part of this land might be requisitioned as a long-term reserve for University building, and asked that the West Burn Lane site should be requisitioned now for the immediate plan. The Trust wrote asking the Council to consider the effects of such a plan on the charm of the historic town centre. The Town Council rejected the Holford plan and suggested the University should build on their own ground in the Canongate.

In August the Town Council amended the Development Plan allocating the West Burn Lane site for the University purposes, and designating for compulsory purchase the part that would be required within ten years. This was not a final decision but the basis for a second Inquiry. In view of representations by the Trust and the National Trust, the Secretary of State reported that he was unable to reconsider his opinion. However, in view of the Franks report there were certain procedures at the recent Inquiry which were at variance with recommendations.

The Second Local Inquiry

This began at the end of November 1956. The Commissioner was Mr T. P. McDonald Q.C. with Sir Patrick Abercrombie as his Planning Adviser. The Inquiry began, was adjourned, and then resumed in February 1957; it was adjourned again. In this interval the death of Sir Patrick Abercrombie occurred. His place was taken by Mr J. M. Aitken, and the Inquiry was resumed in early May. The parties were: Counsel for the University and for a committee of ratepayers; Counsel for the Town Council; Counsel for the proprietors of the site as a group of individual objectors.

The University stated that, if it was not granted the West Burn Lane site, it would be bound to use the Union Street site and the space left between the two main colleges in the historic centre.

The submission by the Trust was concerned solely with the question of amenity and the character of St Andrews.

> The buildings on this site will seriously upset the balance between various interests – academic, business, and domestic in this area of the city which they have shared for so long. The Trust objects to changes in the range of houses which are north of the boundary of the site; this site contains the finest group of old houses which are protected under Town and Country Planning Act 1947. The houses retain their traditional long rigs; they are domestic houses for which there is no parallel in the country or elsewhere in St Andrews. The Trustees are perturbed by the nature of the proposed buildings. Blocks of modern laboratories of such size are quite foreign to the traditional aspect of the site. They would bulk large from the much admired views of the city from the south.

The Trustees then asked, 'Where would the University expand after the site is full? It would be impossible to deny further claims using compulsory purchase orders. It would seem better if the University direct its development to a clear and unhampered site without the city centre. St Andrews is so far relatively small and compact.'

(*I was only able to attend a few hours on some days of the hearings. Feelings ran high; I remember getting on the St Andrews train to go to Dundee. We sat cosily in the carriage facing our fellow travellers. I was with a friend who wrote a note to me; it said, ' Don't bring up THE SUBJECT – those two are on the other side.'*)

There were some entertaining and many interesting passages during the hearings. One contention on behalf of the householders was the preservation of the medieval gardens. It was rather awkward that Dr McKerrow, who lived in one of the houses in South Street, had been given permission to build a house for his retirement in his garden (the long rigg behind his house), and building was well advanced. His son, also a doctor, was to take over the practice house and surgery. The Counsel for the Householders asserted that the University had been aware of their intentions and should have informed Dr McKerrow before building began. It was asserted that Dr McKerrow had spoken about it to Principal Knox one day – 'in the cloakroom at the Royal and Ancient'. The Principal denied that he knew anything of the West Burn Lane Plan at that time. From the dates given, this was scarcely credible.

The Secretary of State's decision on the Inquiry was a great disappointment. He appreciated the considerations of amenity and historical interest put forward by the Trust, but he accepted the Commissioner's view that these considerations were outweighed by the importance of enabling the University to provide facilities for the modern teaching of basic sciences and confirmed his earlier amendment to the Burgh Development Plan. The Trust protested; they were particularly critical of one phrase used by the Commissioner 'the needs of history can be settled by graphical records'. This would negate all the work of Preservation Trusts and other similar bodies. In spite of this protest, and those of the National Trust and both Houses of Parliament, the Secretary of State felt that he was unable to reconsider his opinion.

In early 1958 the Town Council issued compulsory purchase orders to the owners of land on the West Burn Lane site. In May the elections took place, and the new Town Council withdrew the orders. A new Inquiry was ordered under Section 96(4) of the Town and Country Planning Act (1954) to see if the Secretary of State would be justified in directing the Town Council to secure the West Burn Lane Site for the University.

The Third Inquiry, 1958

This was held from the end of September to early October, 1958. The Commissioner was Mr J.O.H. Hunter Q.C. The Trust submitted the statement it had made at the 1956-7 Inquiry. There was a verbal statement from the Town Council.

The outcome was not known until February 1959 when Mr Hunter decided he would not, in the present circumstances, be justified in requiring the Town Council to take the steps of issuing compulsory purchase orders to acquire the land at West Burn Lane. It could not be said the site was adequate in size for the science expansion, and the type of building proposed was considered by him to be unsuitable for this area. If it was the intention of the University to impose a rigid and permanent figure for the number of science students, the Scores area was not eliminated. Also the Playing Fields and Cockshaugh area gave enough room for expansion. By the Franks report, compulsory purchase orders were unjustifiable. It would be an interference of property rights, and the permanent destruction of an area of historical features unique in Scotland and of high amenity value.

There was relief and jubilation for one side, and dismay but also some mixed feelings among the University Staff.

The University announced that the Scores area was not suitable for the erection of science buildings on the scale required, and they would be obliged to send the extra number of science students to Queens College, Dundee. This involved the loss of a large grant to St Andrews. However, Principal Knox seemed to be very ready to keep St Andrews as a small centre of excellence, mainly for the Arts.

In 1960 the University was able to announce its intention to begin building on the North Haugh, and instead of the student numbers rising from 1400 to 2300 as planned, the number could now go up to 2700 as previously proposed. So what turn had the drama taken to bring in this fresh scene? It is said that Professor Wright had been talking to Mr Zander Cheape in the Royal and Ancient clubhouse. The version I heard (very likely apocryphal!) was that Professor Wright had been bemoaning the fact that because another women's residence was needed and there was no land for it, students were living in flats in the town, and there was grave danger of immorality. Mr Cheape owned Strathtyrum, the large estate immediately west of Petherum Bridge. He was so concerned that he said he would consider selling to the Unversity 65 acres of his land on the west of the Town. (I have no doubt that Mr Cheape was fully aware of the critical state regarding university expansion.) Negotiations began at once, and a deal was made.

The first building to be erected on this site was the Andrew Melville Hall of Residence. I don't know what Mr Cheape said, but ironically it was to be the first mixed residence! The architect was Sir James Stirling; the building is described by McWilliam as 'a huge V-shape confidently stepping down the slope in blocks of ribbed concrete articulated by continuous glazing and canted bays'. For years there were drainage problems. The intention was to echo the design of this building in the ensuing science blocks. This fine site is now filled with ill-assorted modern buildings, but the site is not in the Conservation Area. The view from the grand houses in Kennedy Gardens has been scarred. For most of the early Trust members who fought to keep St Andrews beautiful, Death has been timely. Among the founder members, only Ronald Cant lived to see the full impact of the North Haugh; what had been done to St Andrews in the last twenty years grieved him deeply. He said one day, not long before his death, 'You can still see the former beauty of the city if you look in the right places'. That is true; South Street, North Street and the Scores have for the most part, and so far, been saved from being spoiled – but what a battle it has been!

Property, 1953 –66

In 1953 the Trust persuaded the Ministry of Works to repair the West Port, and to take over responsibility for the Priory, which was later put in good order. Also the Town Council agreed to repair the roof of the Oast House at Law Mill. Later the Law Mill Pond, which was filled with mud, was restored through the Trust having the lade leading from the Lumbo Burn cleared. In 1980 the Trust tried unsuccessfully to acquire the cottage and mill from the Town Council; the Town sold it to raise money for the Common Good fund. The cottage is occupied and in good order.

Most buildings cared for by the Trust are dwelling houses, but in 1961 the owner of the Bogward doocot transferred it to the Trust, which accepted responsibility for its maintenance. This 'beehive'-shaped doocot, at the end of the Lade Braes, was probably built by the Priory of St Andrews in the sixteenth century. The building was restored by the Trust with the help of a grant from the Dalrymple Trust. In 1974 some further restoration work was carried out by the Trust; there was damage to the fabric due to water-logging because of building developments. The doocot turned out to be a demanding legacy, and in 1992 there was trouble. The doocot was surrounded by the Bogward estate development, and householders made objections to the number of pigeons (over one thousand) living at the doocot, and their smell. The Trust was advised by the health authority to take a radical step: to carry out a cull and to have the doocot closed. When the men came to carry this out they found a ring of local children round the doocot making a stance to protect the birds. The children had a measure of success: the operation was postponed, but the doocot had to be cleaned and the number of birds drastically reduced.

On several occasions the Trust raised with the Town Council the possibility of its buying South Court, an early 15th-century mansion house with 16th- and 17th-century alterations and additions; as the garden was involved in the West Burn Lane dispute the Council retained the property, and eventually renovated it in 1968-72. This fine piece of work on the Great Eastern and South Court was carried out by W. Murray Jack, the local architect whose plans were so sympathetic to the early vernacular styles. Recently this handsome historic house has had its setting sadly reduced. There was only a small part of the rigg left, and now there is even less due to the rebuilding of the Byre Theatre begun in 1997.

141 South Street, the Burgher Close

In the Close, on the north stands the picturesque early 18th century three-storey house which was used as the second Burgher Meeting House from 1774 to 1786. The Bell family, who had owned it for two hundred years, sold it to the Trust. Miss Low undertook to pay all the costs of restoring it; it was completed in 1963 and let to the Red Cross for their local headquarters. In 1976 a house in Burgher Close was let to Jurek Putter, the graphic artist known for his research into medieval St Andrews and his meticulous large-scale illustrations.

12-20 [sic] **North Street**

Through Miss Low's benefaction for the Burgher House, the Trust was left with funds to acquire a further property. In 1962 they bought two adjacent houses; previously these had been three 18th century pantiled houses reconstructed by Mr James Scott in 1936 as a home for himself. He was now living elsewhere and offered the property to the Trust. The plan was to sell the west part as a separate house and keep the East part (now number 12) for Trust purposes. The Trust had used Mr Gilchrist's office at 90 South Street, and had held meetings in the Hall at Louden's Close. 12 North Street now became the new headquarters. Miss Low paid for the costs of the conversion.

Miss Low died on 20 December 1962; she had been a great benefactor and had participated in the successes of the Trust over the years. She had moved from Blebo House to South Street in 1952, and was Honorary Vice-President from 1956. Her aim was to enable the Trust to move from one project to the next. She was loved and respected by all who knew her.

In 1964 the National Trust gave £1000 per annum for two years, an interest-free loan to the Fife County Council for projects connected with the St Andrews Preservation Trust. In 1965 Miss Dorothy Bryson left £6000 to the Trust. Later Dr J.B. Ritchie left a legacy of £50,000 to the Trust.

Zoning

In 1961 there were Preservation Trusts at Crail and at Ceres, and these two societies and the St Andrews one took over responsibility for adjacent parishes – in the case of St Andrews, Leuchars, Dunino, Cameron, and Kingsbarns. Hayswell Cottage, the old building to the north of the Norman church at Leuchars was in need of repair. The Trust took it over and eventually sold it to a buyer who put it in good order.

11 College Street

In 1966 the Trust acquired this important property. The building dates from the sixteenth century and its rehabilitation was urgent. The project was costly, but fortunately the Trust had just received a generous bequest of over £6000 from Miss Dorothy Bryson. The building was sold in 1971. It and the two old houses at the north end of College Street add to the atmosphere of this wynd leading to the United College.

Victorian buildings

The Trust succeeded in having preservation orders put on some of the handsome Victorian and Edwardian houses in St Andrews.

Historic Monuments

In addition to the buildings which it preserved itself, the Trust took every opportunity to ensure the preservation of historic structures in

St Andrews. Under the Ancient Monuments Acts, the Ministry of Works maintained the cathedral and castle in excellent order, and since 1948 – following a suggestion by the Trust – the Priory and the West Port. The latter was thoroughly repaired by expert craftsmen, and work was done at the Priory. The Trustees were happy to help with this work, using a donation from the Kate Kennedy Club in 1959 to provide four seats in the cloister. In 1957, at the Blackfriars Chapel, which had been taken over by the Ministry several years earlier, the Trust helped the Town Council to improve the surroundings by the provision of a railing and by planting flowers. It was also instrumental in persuading the Ministry to provide more informative notices here and at St Mary's church, Kirkhill.

The Trust was also influential in promoting the repair in 1967 of the fine medieval bridge at Guard Bridge (by the Ministry and Fife Council). The Trust itself undertook the repair of the monuments to Archbishop Sharp and the Covenanters at Magus Muir.

Publications

One of the aspects of the work of the Trust was the production of publications. These small books have been both useful and popular. The titles are: *Old St Andrews: the Handbook of the St Andrews Preservation Trust*; *Georgian and Early Victorian St Andrews*; *Conservation and the Work of the Trust 1937-1975*. In 1958 the fourth Trust publication appeared: *Trees in St Andrews* by Dr J.A. Macdonald. The Trust Handbook was revised from time to time. Each Annual Report contained a contributed article (many by Dr Ronald Cant). In 1992 a selection of these articles was published under the title *Three Decades of Historical Notes (1964-1989)* edited by Miss Mary Innes and Dr Joan Whelan. Miss Innes died just after completing this valuable work.

Trees

The Trust book on trees raised a lot of interest. By 1962 one hundred trees had been planted. There was still great concern about the 'mutilation of trees and the destruction of trees', and a demonstration of pruning was held. In 1963 the Law Park wood was given to the Trust by Philip Boase in memory of his brother Norman Boase, together with money for its upkeep for seven years.

The Trustees showed great concern about the loss of good trees and the severe lopping which took place over the years. They were also the donors of many trees, and the instigators of donations from individuals. Trees were planted at Langlands School, New Park School, the Lade Braes; at the West Cemetery; at Greyfriars Garden and Queens Gardens; at West Acres; a flowering cherry at South Court; Jersey elms in the avenue at St Leonards Chapel; also at Priestden Den, and on the roads into St Andrews from Largo and from Ceres. In 1964 Mr Philip Boase, Mr David Hardie and Mr S.L. Mowat made a survey of trees.

The work of guarding mature trees and of planting trees has continued. In 1974 a party cleared up the Law Park wood (called the Boase Wood) and made fresh plantings. Subsequently many bulbs were planted. This wood was again in need of clearing up in 1980, and through Professor J.F. Allen the M.S.C. arranged for work to be done under the Youth Employment Scheme. Later the New Park schoolboys planted bulbs and tidied the wood. This caring work of clearance, replanting and tidying has continued over the years. Three students from the Geology Department plotted the trees in Boase Wood, and careful records were kept. In 1988 eighteen damaged trees had to be removed from Boase wood, and were replaced by red oak, rowan, ash and birch. Mrs Berit Owen and friends made a tree nursery and set young trees out in gap sites over a wide area of the East Neuk.

In 1976 the limes in South Street which had been planted in 1879 had to be replaced; the Trust shared the cost with the District Council.

In 1980 several elm trees were lost through Dutch elm disease. The old mulberry tree (some said it was two hundred years old) to the north of the Byre died in 1984 and the Trust planted two new ones which have flourished. The Tree Committee continued to carry out its objective 'to ensure a city of trees for future generations'.

Amenity Problems

The appearance of an old town derives its distinctive quality from many features, and the Trustees gave attention to these. For example, they urged that the design of shop signboards, directions boards and 'street furniture' should be as simple and dignified as possible. The switch from gas lighting to electric lighting in 1960 brought problems about the use of unattractive swan-necked fitments to the traditional standards. The Trust advocated the use of bracket lanterns, and some made by Mr Harvey, the blacksmith, were fitted to standards in Louden's Close and Crail's Lane. The Trust asked that such fitments be made to the lights in the Pends, at the Harbour and in the Abbotsford Crescent area. In 1965 the Trust objected to new standards to be put in Market Street, Bell Street, Church Street and Greyfriars Garden, which were 35 feet high, but these were fitted and gave very good lighting.

Planning and Developments

In 1958 the Trust made strong protests – in vain – at the proposed demolition of the Bank of Scotland on the corner of South Street and Queens Gardens. This was a Peddie and Kinnear building of 1871. It was demolished in 1960 and replaced by a classical modern building, but the Trust had managed to get an agreement that it would be faced with sandstone. (*The flat roof of this Bank has always seemed to me inappropriate in the setting. Now in 2002 there is a plan to replace it:*

developers intend to build flats for student occupation. The Trust showed concern, and the plan was withdrawn pro-tem.)

The Bus Garage and Bus Station

The Trust objected to the plans for the garage; it was to be in an exposed position beside the railway station, and of a large size, and it would entail the cutting down of good trees. Some adaptations were made to the size and design, and it was useful to the Town to have a bus station instead of using stances in South Street. A small bus shelter designed by the Trust was erected in Abbey Street.

Traffic

There was concern about the noise and the speed of traffic on the main roads of St Andrews, and it was suggested that a speed limit of twenty miles an hour should be introduced. This has not happened in spite of repeated requests, and, at the time of writing (April 2000), the same demand is being made! In the Summer of 1964 parking difficulties were discussed. Eventually paid parking was introduced in 1991. In 1976 a public meeting was called with regard to the threat to the Town Centre by traffic. The proposal to remove the bandstand in the Scores to make a parking place was successfully opposed by the Trust. It was agreed that the Trust would keep the Bandstand in good order. It was repainted, and a splendid concert was given by the Madras School Band. (In recent years there has been a series of concerts on Sunday afternoons in the summer.)

A Run of Developments

The British Railway Hotel

The Trustees studied the plans for this hotel which was to be built by the railway goods station. The hotel was to be of a considerable size, and the Trust was greatly concerned by its design in relation to its surroundings.

It was described by one local as 'a large concrete chest with its drawers all pulled out' (these were the balconies on the north side). It is indeed unfortunate that the plans for this flat-roofed building were accepted by the Council. The developers held out a carrot: the local Leuchars-St Andrews branch line was threatened with closure, and it was believed that if a railway hotel was built the rail link must be retained. But Beeching was ruthless; the day the hotel was opened on 25 June 1968, the rails of the branch line were being torn up. The Hotel changed hands. In 1978 there was a petition against the Old Course Hotel Trusts regarding plans to add wings; there were three thousand signatures and it had the support of all the local bodies. On 8 June the District Council granted outline permission: 'We are assured that the British Trust Hotels are determined to avoid inflicting another architectural disaster on the town.' In 1982 the Preservation Trust again made objections to proposed additions as 'altogether too massive'. It is amazing to report that in this the year 2000, in preparation for the Millenium Open Golf Championship here, a further extension was erected; it is said that it ruins the line of the seventeenth hole. The sprawling hybrid is unsuited to its unique site, although I suppose it must be good to stay there and enjoy its luxuries, but its views are not what they used to be (see below). The current top price for bed and breakfast in the Royal Suite is £575 but, as Michael Tobert wrote in his book *Pilgrims in the Rough*, 'You can slum it at the back for a trifling £270'.

Abbey Street, 1966

The group of old houses at the foot of the South Court rigg had been derelict for years. The Town Council carried out the demolition. In 1968 the new Byre Theatre was planned; the Trust asked if some of the features of the old Byre might be retained. The incorporation of the doocot from the old barn was a nice touch. The Trustees were unhappy about the quality of the proposed building and asked if the development could be kept in scale and character with the surroundings. Unfortunately the scheme was subject to restriction.

The building met with a favourable response. In 1997 it was demolished, to the dismay of many. A much more spacious new Byre theatre is well on the way through the award of Lottery funds, but costs have escalated.

In 1969 the development of the south-west side of Abbey Street was completed; the scheme provided Council flats for a number of elderly people and won an award for its design. The buildings on the east side of the street, which included an old inn, had been demolished to widen the road. A fine stretch of the St Leonards (the Priory) wall was revealed. Dauphin House was saved by a remarkable piece of engineering work. When the round tower and part of wall opposite Dauphin Hill were taken down, each stone was marked; then the wall and tower were re-erected several feet back. I watched this work and rejoiced in how well it was carried out and how good it looks, with green grass and rose beds in front of it. The road is two-lane as the Trust hoped. Just as remarkable as the moving of the wall was the salvation of 24 South Street which was to be removed to make a wider entry from Abbey Street into South Street. It is a late sixteenth or early seventeenth century building. A false front had been built on to it. Mr W. Murray Jack made sketch plans for its reconstruction. He proved that the removal of the present frontage would make the road wide enough to satisfy specifications. The Town Council agreed to allow the Trust to buy the house and carry out this plan, and was prepared to advance the cost of the rehabilitation until the Trust could repay it. (This they did, on the sale of 11 College Street.) The plans involved extensive work, so the Council gave a Discretionary Improvement grant of £1200. The Plan also meant that the widened Abbey Street joined South Street at a more acceptable angle. 24 South Street was sold in 1972. Mr Jack was awarded an honour for the design; he received it at Holyrood on 24 June 1975 and on the following day the Queen Mother visited St Andrews. Mr Jack and A.B. Paterson showed her over the house. The Queen Mother also visited the Trust's headquarters at 12 North Street.

Another Doocot

In 1983 the Trust wanted to turn its attention to a new project. It bought from Mr Roger the doocot at Kenley Green which was in dire need of repair. Historic Buildings offered a grant but the Trust could not meet the costs of the extent of repairs suggested, so had to turn it down. Essential repairs to the roof were carried out in two phases. Over the next years, this doocot was put into good order.

Objections to Developments

The West Park Hotel

In 1966 the University put out plans for a new students Union to be built in St Mary's Place. This involved an appeal against the demolition of the West Park Hotel, a David Bryce building of 1866: 'The Trust regrets the loss of the amenity value of the quiet dignity of the Hotel and its grounds. It has doubts as to the covering of the whole site with buildings. It deplores the assertiveness of the St Mary's Street facade of the new structure with its oversailing first and second floors.' The University considered the Trust's comments but stuck to the plans. The intrusion altered the facade of Market Street; if you stand across the road to the west of Alexandra Place and Hope Park, it is sad to see this concrete and glass construction obtrude among the elegant sandstone buildings. Formerly you saw St Salvator's tower from this corner. West Park might have been part of the new Union buildings; if this was not possible, the Union could have been built some yards to the north, with trees and grass on the street side. The placing was crucial; remember that Sir James Irvine managed to have the Younger Hall set back from the street frontage, and the new University Library is not part of the North Street frontage.

The Trust, the Town Council and the University

In the mid-sixties the Town Council had failed to make draft plan applications for development available to the Trust, so that any objections or suggestions made by the Trust came too late. The Council agreed that a representative of the Trust should attend planning meetings; this proved helpful. It was also agreed later that there would be a quarterly meeting between representatives of the Trust and of the Council. A minute was sent to the University asking that the Principal should attend the committee meetings of the Trustees or send a representative. There is a note in the 1972 report that Principal Steven Watson at a Trust meeting 'gave the Trustees a very frank review of the University's building plans'. In 1971 the old city was designated as a conservation area. The Trust advised 'every effort must be made to focus public attention upon matters which affect the future development of St Andrews'. It was helpful to the Trust's work that, in the Town and Country Planning (Amendment Act 1972) Historic buildings in the Conservation area, there was a clause: 'notification of consent to demolish a listed building should be given to the Scottish Civic Trust, the Georgian Society, R.C.A.H.M.S. and local amenity societies. The Secretary of State must have the comments of these bodies before giving consent.'

Property

Logies Lane

The Town Council gave the Trust the opportunity of making observations on the plans submitted by Boots for reconstruction of the Logies Lane property so that the City Arms could be incorporated into Boots. An excellent conversion was made and Church Square was enhanced.

The Trust acquired the Brand house at the south end of Fleming Place with a view to restoration, and found a purchaser who was ready to undertake the work according to the Trust specifications.

The University Arts Centre

At a meeting with Vice-Principal Lionel Butler to discuss the plans for this Centre, the Trust put forward suggestions about lowering the height of the drama studio and the extension.

Other Property

Professor Alan Boase gave the Trust the feu rights to land at ***the*** *Taft, Hepburn Gardens,* so that it had control over any future developments. The Trust objected to plans by Guardo Investments for the development of *177-187 South Street;* some modifications were made. Objections were also made to plans to make *99 North Street* into a theatre changing rooms and workshop; the Town Council refused permission.

Changes in Local Government

On 16 May 1974 came news of very important changes. The Town Council function as local authority and planning authority was to be taken over by the North East Fife District Council. The last meeting of the St Andrews Town Council was held on 10 May 1975. Gone were our Provost, our magistrates, our Bailies and the ancient traditions. And gone was close co-operation between the Trust and the Town Council's planning committee. However, the Director of Physical Planning, Mr Philip Hutchison, worked with a sympathetic understanding of the particular needs of and threats to St Andrews.

Pressure from Developers

Mr Shields and Professor J.F. Allen scanned lists of applications for building in the St Andrews area which were sent weekly to the Trust; they visited the sites and put forward information for discussion with the Trustees. This work was critical, and became increasingly demanding.

Balone Farm

In 1977 Wimpey and Co. submitted plans for a housing development at Balone Farm. There was a Public Inquiry, and the Trust presented an independent case. It rested on the argument 'because of its situation and its beauty St Andrews is particularly vulnerable to uncontrolled ribbon development, and its growth should be limited to that generated by the increase of permanent local employment'. On the findings the application was turned down.

Public Inquiry into the St Andrews Local Plan, June 1982

Dr Brooks spoke for the Trust. The Reporter supported the following recommendations put forward by the Trust:

1. That developments to the south and west of the town should be severely restricted.
2. That the conservation area should be extended.
3. *Re* the introduction of a new traffic management scheme: there should be a one-way flow of traffic through the West Port.
4. The Bruce Embankment should be abandoned as a site for a new swimming pool in favour of the St Nicholas site. Subsequently a well-designed Leisure Centre was built at the St Nicholas site.
5. *Re* the Brownhills Caravan site: that a policy of planting should be adopted at the caravan site to screen it.

In 1984 the Trust made strong objections to changes at the Brownhills Caravan site. This site had belonged to the Town Council and was run as a summer site only. All caravans were removed at the end of each summer. Then it was sold to a company, and caravans were allowed to remain there all the year round. 'It had previously been a temporary eye-sore in the summer months; now it was a chalet village with a public house.' (*It has since spread even more and covers a large and prominent area – it can be seen from miles away along the coast. It is indeed an eyesore, yet it fulfils a need.*)

Plans opposed by the Trust, 1985-1988

An application to develop the Old Cinema House into a Dance Hall/Amusement Centre was opposed. The cinema was demolished to make way for a block of flats; the Trust regretted the loss of the period decor.

Applications were made for the holding of fun fairs during the summer on the West Sands; this was refused by the Council, it being 'a designated area of great landscape value'.

The Trust successfully supported plans to develop sheltered housing at the Argyle Street Brewery, in preference to an application for a William Low supermarket.

The Death of Miss Annabel Kidston

The address at her funeral service at St Leonard's on 19 February 1982 is given in the Trust Report. She was born in 1896 and came to St Andrews in 1936 to join her sister Margaret, a lecturer in the Anatomy Department. During the War she taught at the Dundee School of Art, and in addition held classes for members of the Polish troops stationed in St Andrews. In 1945 she moved from Bank House in College Street to 12 Howard Place. 'She was the moving spirit of the founding of the St Andrews Preservation Trust, which was a pioneer movement of this nature in Scotland. She was a source of ceaseless activity in her painting and in her work for the Trust. She played a remarkably effective part wherever she might be in cultural life. In 1965 she bought and restored 21 Market Street for herself and the next door house, number 23, for her sister Nell. In her last years she continued to build up the Trust records.'

Local Plan

The Draft Local plan for the St Andrews area came out in March 1981, and there was a Public Inquiry in June 1982 which went on for a week. The heartening result was – in a nutshell – 'to prevent unbalanced urban sprawl there should be no development to the south west of St Andrews. Accordingly the N E F D C turned down the proposed Craigton Road development.' In 1985 a further plan to build on both sides of the Craigton Road was submitted and refused. It seemed that clear town boundaries were established.

Trust Properties, 1982

Many houses had been saved; the Trust had raised the rents to a more realistic level in 1982. However, this still did not meet the costs of repairs, and it was decided to sell the properties; they were all listed buildings and therefore secure. The little houses were sold by 1988.

The Trust now centred its work on the above-mentioned project of the doocot at Kenley Green, its Museum (the story of which comes later), and the erection of plaques on those houses where noted citizens had lived. The last of these was organised by Professor J.F. Allen. Time and energy went into the increasing battle to protect St Andrews from being swamped by development which would change its whole character.

In 1985 objections were made to an application by Lauders, 116

South Street, to build an extension on the long rigg for use as a Night Club. There was an Inquiry, and the application was turned down.

Losses

In March 1989 the Trust had news of the death of Mr Alexander Gilchrist at the age of 96. He had been Secretary to the Trust from its founding until 1966. One story will illustrate his character. Three elderly sisters lived in the tall house on the south-east side of the West Port. Mr Gilchrist's office (and those of the Trust for many years) was at 90 South Street. On his way home every day he propped his bicycle by the door of this house and went in to do a good turn for the rather frail ladies: he carried buckets of coal from the cellar up two flights to the drawing room. (*I went to look at this house when it was for sale after the death of the third sister. In the scullery there was a gas bracket on which were strung a line of wishbones – the old ladies had not got round to pulling them. This house and the old Bluebell Hotel next door are now the West Port Hotel.*)

At the end of October 1989 came the greatly mourned death of Mr A.B. Paterson, a founder member of the Trust and a former Chairman. In his funeral oration he was termed 'Mr St Andrews'. There could not have been a greater and more apt compliment.

Officers and Committees

From 1958 to 1971 Dr Hew Lorimer of Kellie Castle, the well-known sculptor represented the National Trust on the St Andrews Preservation Trust Committee and formed strong and useful bonds. He was Chairman of the Trustees from 1966 to 1971, the longest time for anyone to hold this office. When he resigned from it he became Honorary Vice Chairman.

Mr A.B Paterson took his place for the next five years, and was succeeded by Dr Nicholas Brooks. Mr Ken Hayward was the Chairman. Mr W.A. Heath held this office from 1982-1985, and Dr W. Buchanan for the next two years.

Mrs E.V.W. Proudfoot, archaeologist a President of the Council for Scottish Archaeology, chaired the Preservation Trust during the difficult years 1988-1992.

The various subcommittees were each headed by a convener. In the nineties these committees were: Finance and Property; Planning; Museum; Publications and Publicity; Tree Committee; also a Green Belt committee was formed with Robert Murray as Chair (it later became the Green Belt Forum; see Chapter 7). Publicity became Publicity and Programmes. From its beginnings the Trustees organised an annual outing, a visit to a place of interest, lectures by visiting speakers, and occasional social events. A grand party was held in the garden of Mrs Pirie's West House in 1997 to celebrate the Trust's sixtieth anniversary.

Recording by the Trust

One of the first actions by the founders of the Trust, in 1937, was to arrange for a photographic survey of the most interesting buildings in St Andrews, particularly the smaller houses under threat of demolition. In 1940-41, after the outbreak of the war, the Trustees carried out as systematic a recording as possible – by means of photographs and measured drawings – of the architecture of the city, and everything was duplicated on microfilm as a security measure. Much of the work was undertaken in co-operation with the National Buildings Record set up in 1940 by the Ministry of Works.

This project, begun as an emergency measure, was continued in succeeding years, and some amateur photographers contributed to it. Older prints and photographs were also added to the Trust's collection.

Chapter 6

THE ST ANDREWS PRESERVATION TRUST MUSEUM

For many years the Trust received legacies and gifts, and acquired artifacts which were related to the social history of St Andrews. Up to 1982 there were only two Museums in St Andrews, one at the Cathedral, and a natural history museum (seldom open to the public), the Bell Pettigrew in the University's Bute Building. In compiling this brief account I have taken most of my information from the section 'Museum Committee' in the *Annual Reports and Year Books* of the Preservation Trust.

One of the core members of the Trust was Mrs Nell Skinner, a remarkable person. When I first knew her she lived with her daughter Mary in Wardlaw Gardens. We used to meet at the Sunday morning service at St Leonard's Church. Nell made a bustling determined entry to the church – she was very lame in one leg, but totally disregarded it. She had also lost the sight of one eye but, nothing daunted, she was wholeheartedly into everything. Around 1962 she bought 36 North Street; it was in poor repair. She had extensive work done and made it her home. (*One day she invited me to tea. She came to the front door, greeted me and said, 'We'll go up to the drawing room'. To my amazement she turned sideways at the staircase, and was suddenly seated and hurling upwards, still talking. I had never seen a stair lift.*)

Nell is described in a short obituary in the Trust report for 1984 as one who maintained 'a steadfast refusal to be daunted by difficulties or discouragements'. For sixteen years she organised (latterly with Gillian Falconer and others) a series of annual summer exhibitions at the Trust House at 12 North Street. The aim was to remind the visitor of the special qualities of everyday life in earlier times, and to emphasise the importance of ensuring that all aspects of it were, as far as possible, conserved for future generations. The exhibitions were amazingly varied. If she was not an expert in any subject, she mastered it. This is a list of some of the themes through the years from 1965: 'Victoriana'; 'Old Scottish Pottery'; 'Weights and Measures'; 'Railways' and 'Writing Materials of the 18th and 19th centuries'; Old Weapons' and 'Ancient Scottish Tartans'; 'Items from the Macgregor Bequest'; 'British Heraldry and Heraldic Embroidery'; 'The Linen Trade' and 'Costumes'; 'Painted Bowls' and 'Antique Playing Cards'; 'Toys and Dolls'; 'Royal Occasions'; 'Tea and Tobacco'; 'Sails and Veils' and a display of twenty three wedding dresses. I remember one of the wedding dresses vividly; it was that of Lady Griselda Cheape of Strathtyrum; it had been 'created' by the Fairfield Stores, and was heavily adorned with beads, lace and ribbons. It might be said that it was heavily oversubscribed. The titles of the last of this series was 'Nursery Days and Cycling Ways 1820-1921'; 'History of the Linen Trade' and 'Patchwork Quilts'.

1974 was European Heritage Year and exhibitions were mounted by Mrs Skinner and Trust members. 'The Architecture of St Andrews' with two hundred photographs from the collection and other illustrations was held in four classrooms at the (old) West Infants School. This was open each afternoon except Saturdays from 7 July to 24 August. At St Leonards School the themes were '18th and 19th century and Edwardian Period Pieces' and 'Charles Rennie Macintosh', open from 25 August to 12 September. And at 12 North Street from mid-July to mid-September there was 'The Linen Trade in Fife' and 'Costumes'. Surely this was a triumph of organisation and powers of persuasion!

Through the years the objective of the Trust was to set up a small permanent museum. In the Annual Reports are acknowledgements of an increasing accumulation of bequests. By 1986 the collection filled (or had filled) the cellar at 141 South Street, a room at Louden's Close, a room at the Burgher Close house, one of the temporary classrooms at the Greyfriars School in Abbey Walk, and space in the Abbey Street Pottery. There was a crisis when the pottery room was needed for other uses. A solution was found: the Church of Scotland General Trustees offered to let the Trust use the empty church of St Mary's, Dairsie as a store, for a nominal rental, and the Trust was to pay rates and insurance cover. This was very helpful, but eventually the distance made it rather awkward. One year a gale blew open a door; nothing was damaged, but the collection there became a source of anxiety. When the Trust offices were established at 14 Queens Gardens it was possible to obtain a further storage room on the ground floor. So in 1996 a grand removal took place of all the precious collection in Dairsie Church. In the Annual Report Miss Gillian Falconer thanks the removal team for supplying 'willingness, trailers and muscles to help'. Over the years the original catalogue cards have been entered on to the database; this work continues.

In 1981 the last of the series of exhibitions recorded above took place. For some time plans had been made for 12 North Street to become a small house museum. This Museum was officially constituted in 1977. John di Folco undertook to organise this; he made all the necessary preparations with the help of Mr Richard McKenzie, who was engaged as a curatorial assistant by arrangement with the Manpower Services Commission. On 5 July 1982 the official opening took place. It was a day of achievement and rejoicing. The theme of the exhibition was 'Social and Community Life in Bygone Days'.

The first full summer season was in 1983; the Museum was open each afternoon (this is still the practice). The season brought 2000 visitors. The running has always depended on the help of volunteers. Dr Nicholas Brookes took over from John di Folco as Museum Convener. For the next four years the Trust Museum had invaluable professional help from a series of assistants from the Manpower Services Commission. Mrs Beryl Neale succeeded Mr Richard

McKenzie. The themes of the first full summer season were: 'St Andrews as a Bathing Resort' and 'Football History of St Andrews'. One of the Museum's larger acquisitions was set up as a permanent exhibit. This was donated by Mr McKechnie in 1977 and comprised the (*circa* 1895) fitments and contents of a St Andrews Victorian chemist's shop. 141 South Street was originally the premises of Smith and Govan's apothecary, then J.D. Kirk took over as chemist at 73 South Street. His assistant dispenser A.W. Keith succeeded him in 1936. The museum display includes sets of old glass bottles, the two enormous carboys which used to dominate the curved window of the shop, an archaic pill-making tool – and more!

Mrs Neale made showcases, and also enabled the reconstruction of the Aikman and Terras shop in the Museum. It was on the south-west corner of Bell Street (occupied now by 'Simply Scotland'). I have already described the shop. Each time I see the dummy figure of the assistant in the Museum set-up, I am back in time, seated and giving my order, approving each item as it is placed on the counter.

1984 was the year of an Open Golf Championship here, and a display on golf ball manufacturers was mounted together with 'Costumes 1860-1930'. In 1985 the Museum was open from l July to 3 September, and also at Easter; for many years there has been a November St Andrews Day exhibition, lately continuing for as long as a week. The themes were: at Easter 'Raisin Receipts'; in the summer, post cards, books and personal items of Martin Anderson (Cynicus) of Leuchars, and 'Communion Tokens'. There were 4385 visitors! When one considers how small the premises are – two rooms upstairs and two down, part of one of these being a small shop – the numbers must have been hard to manage.

In 1986 Mr J.L. Hunter Scott was Museum Convener, and in his absence abroad Mrs E.V.W. Proudfoot deputised. The curatorial assistant was Mr Sweet. It was necessary to close the Museum at the end of August, due to a change of rules by the M.S.C. Certain restrictions were placed on the range of work of its museum assistants;

they must no longer act as guides, and they must not take money. This undermined the usefulness of what had been valuable appointments.

In 1987 Mrs Marion Wood was part-time professional curator. The curator selected and was responsible for researching and mounting exhibitions. (Mrs Wood left in 1990, and now runs the Museum at Kinburn.) The exhibitions were 'Pictures by Local Artists' and 'Local Archaeology'. The number of visitors increased to 4700.

In 1988 the Museum became free to visitors – who numbered 5350. The exhibitions were 'Picture Postcards of St Andrews', 'Local Archaeology' and 'Paintings by Local Artists'.

In 1989 the Museum was open at Easter and for July, August and September. The exhibition was 'Paintings by Local Artists from the Trust's Collection'. There were 4842 visitors. A series of seminars for assistant volunteers was well attended and found to be helpful.

For some time the North East Fife District Council had been hoping to establish a museum at St Andrews. There were plans to set it up at Kinburn House. This brought debate regarding the future of the Trust Museum. It had been tacitly assumed by the Trustees that in this event the Trust Museum's collection would come under the Council. A meeting was held with members of the District Council's Parks and Recreation department to consider the sharing of resources; the results were described as 'inconclusive'. Increasingly it became apparent that the Trust would find it difficult to work in partnership with the Council. At a special meeting of members of the Preservation Trust in March it was unanimously decided that the Trust should retain its Museum at 12 North Street as a Museum of St Andrews. It was considered advisable to register for approval under the Museum and Galleries Act. This would mean that it would be eligible for grants. The need for a full-time curator was evident. Eventually a mutual loan scheme was worked out between the two museums and associates, and there is now a very good relationship with the Council Museum Service which gives a lot of help and support.

In 1990 Gareth Russell was the assistant. In the summer, besides repeat exhibitions, there was also a delightful small exhibition of paper-weights organised by Mary Innes. The St Andrews Day exhibition illustrated conservation in St Andrews by means of pictures from the Trust collection. Visitor numbers were 3780.

In 1991 the Museum was open from mid-June to mid-September and in addition at Easter and on St Andrews Day, and by appointment for schools, other groups and academic visitors (a total of 4258 for the year). For the first time the Trust had appointed a full-time professional curator, Miss Jo Lynn. The Convener wrote 'her unenviable task was to complete the cataloguing, ensure artifacts were in the correct places, and those in need of conservation identified. She also supervised the first 'museum-clean' for some years, including the store at Dairsie.

In addition, some useful work was done by two students from the Arts and Museum Course at the University. Miss C. Pittaway studied the storage and conservation needs of the Trust's collection of photographs, and made useful recommendations which were followed up. Miss Anna Robertson prepared work sheets for visiting school groups. From the report: 'an ongoing enjoyable series of scrap book working parties has produced records which are valuable and are popular with visitors' . (The original donated scrap-books which had inspired this annual work were those of Mr George Cowie, the photographer, and the Macgregor scrap books.) The two summer exhibitions were: one on 'Mr Harvey and local blacksmith work', and the other by Miss Betty Bushnell on her collection of 'Crest China'. There was a significant increase in donations.

In 1992 Ruth Neave became curator. Mrs Proudfoot stood down as Chairman of the Trustees and became Convener of the Museum Committee. For the previous two years the Committee had spent much time on preparing for the Museum Registration Scheme. A new Collections and Disposals policy had been prepared for ratification at the A.G.M. The submission was made in 1992, and full registration was given two years later.

The matter of a Museum extension had been discussed for some time; office and working space were urgently needed. Plans drawn up by Michael Scott indicated that the costs involved would be about £150,000. Historic Scotland offered £2500, N.E. Fife Council £500 and Fife Region £1000. This extension would be built on the ground immediately behind the Museum which the Trust had bought from the Castle Tavern with this plan in mind. An archaeological excavation of the ground proceeded; old china and a brass pot were discovered.

In this year it was possible to open the Museum every afternoon from Easter to October. Exhibitions were 'Wilson's Bottling Plant', 'Carpentry Tools'and 'Crest China'. There were 4640 visitors.

In 1993 the exhibitions were 'The Unsung Heroes, the Use of Horses in St Andrews' and 'Paintings by Peter Graham R.A.' He was from a local family and was a landscape painter of the West Highlands. The numbers were up to 5706.

In 1994 a fund-raising target of £180,000 was set for the purpose of building the extension to the museum, and an appeal was launched. The plans had been amended to a one-storey building and had been approved. The Scottish Museum had offered a grant of £45,000 towards the costs. There were some doubts about the viability of a museum extension.

The exhibitions set up by the Ruth Neave and students were: 'Pastimes in Past Times' and 'A Day at the Seaside'.

In 1995 the new curator was Mrs Emily Cook and the convener was Miss Gillian Falconer. This year an entrance fee was tried, but it proved counterproductive. The numbers went down to 2360. The exhibitions were 'The Story of the Cinema' which included Miss Ada Walker's paintings from the New Cinema House, and 'Dentistry'. This year a difficult and important decision was made: that the Trust would not proceed with the proposed Museum extension. The difficulty was that, in view of possible legal expenses regarding the applications for large developments, it would be unwise to embark on such an outlay. There had been a handsome legacy from Miss Molly

D'Arcy Thompson, and it was decided to create a D'Arcy Thompson Garden behind the Museum. Gillian Falconer and Penny Fraser were the leaders in this project. A paved area was laid down with help from BBC's Beechgrove Garden. This and the flower garden and the open exhibition gallery made a pleasing and useful extension to the museum; they were opened in 1998.

1996: Free entrance was restored, and the entry figures went up to 5527. The exhibitions were: at Easter, 'The Farms of St Andrews', and in the summer 'On Foreign Soil' (the Polish Forces in St Andrews 1940-45).

1997: The summer exhibition was 'Set in Stone' which illustrated how the town and buildings had changed. It also included models which displayed medieval, Victorian and modern clothes; many of the model stands were constructed by Gillian Falconer. In her report she wonders how many visitors from abroad took home photographs of 'the splendid 1374 pilgrim'. The November exhibition was targeted at increasing public awareness about the need for a green belt at for St Andrews. Numbers were 4900.

1998: Matthew Jarron became curator. The Easter exhibition was called, 'A Journey through the Lade Braes'; this was later removed to the very useful new exhibition shelter in the garden which was opened in June 1988. The summer exhibition was 'Jam Jars and Movie Stars – the Story of the Cinema in St Andrews'. In November we had 'St Andrews Through the Lens' (rare photos from the Museum's collection plus new ones commissioned from young photographer Stephen Robinson) which illustrated how the town and the buildings of St Andrews had changed. The numbers went up to 8119.

1999: In March 'Timeless Tide', an exhibition of art and sculpture by professional artists, was organised by students. The Easter exhibition was 'Every Home Comfort – Hotels in St Andrews', which later took its turn in the garden gallery. In the summer, locals and tourists enjoyed 'End of the Line: A History of the St Andrews and Fife Coast Railways' with an excellent video, and a talk (repeated by request) by Matthew Jarron 'Steam on the Screen'. With the help of a 50% grant from the Scottish Museum's Council, a permanent feature, 'Great Grannie's Washhouse', was set up in the garden shed next to the Open Display area. November featured ' David Niven: A Life in St Andrews'. David was known to everyone, as a merchant, citizen, Provost of St Andrews, later Chairman of the District Council and M.B.E. The visitor figures this year were 9836. Two film crews made use of the premises. Both this year and last year the Trust garden was open as one of 'The Hidden Gardens of St Andrews' and refreshments were served all day. The garden won an award in the Fife Council Annual Garden Competition.

The number of visitors increases annually. Matthew put on an unprecedented number of five exhibitions in 2000: in February-March 'Circa', an exhibition of student art; at Easter 'St Andrews 2000'; the summer exhibition was 'The Best Years of Your Life? Schools in St Andrews'. This was very popular with young and old. There were an amazing number of school photographs, contributions by contemporary schoolchildren and a fascinating video of St Leonards School made in 1937. Then there was 'Between the Lines', an exhibition to be put on by STANZA Poetry Festival, an exciting annual St Andrews early October event. The figures for visitors to the Museum for 2000 were over 10,000.

Matthew Jarron was appointed to the post of Curator at Dundee University. His successor, Susan Keracher, is a St Andrean – a former pupil of Madras College and a graduate of the University Department of Art History. She has researched and mounted these excellent exhibitions: in October 2000 'Unseen St Andrews' (photographs by Willie Patrick and Andrew Cowie); in February 2001 an exhibition of Ruth Walker's paintings (Ruth was art teacher at St Leonards School and is a well-known artist); at Easter 2001 'St Andrews Women' – a group of people who were benefactors to the town; in the summer 'Window Shopping', showing shops now gone but familiar to many of us; in November 'Prints and Drawings by Malcolm Paterson'. Many students of my time and later would leave here with a print by Malcolm Paterson. (In 1970 I bought Orchard Cottage in Greenside Place, where his daughter, a librarian at the old University Library had lived; before that the family lived at Dauphin House nearby.)

That is the outline of a success story. The thousands of hours of planning, of co-operation, of hard work have overcome difficulties and made the little museum one of the features of St Andrews. So much of the past has been saved. So many thousands of people have found interest and pleasure, not least perhaps the comparatively small number of Trust members and others who have given their time. And much is owed, too, to the succession of professional curators who have made an invaluable contribution through their expertise, their research and their commitment.

The Hidden Gardens of St Andrews

The National Open Gardens Scheme has proved such a success that in 1997 Mrs June Baxter discussed with the committee of the St Andrews Preservation Trust whether they might hold a similar day in St Andrews. It was agreed that they would, and a date was chosen and arrangements were made. On the first occasion the money raised went to the Gardens Scheme, but since then it has gone to the funds of the Preservation Trust, averaging £4000 each year and rising to £4900 in the year 2001. It is a popular event and so far we have been lucky with the weather. One favourite is June Baxter's long rigg garden at 46 South Street, where teas are served, and a central feature has been Penny Uprichard's amazing hat stall which looked, from a distance, like a raised blossom-filled flower bed. Other garden owners also offered refreshments, including the Trust Museum garden which, in 1999, won an award in the Fife Council Annual Garden Competition. Its success is due to Gillian Falconer and others for their inspiration and their work.

Chapter 7

THE GATHERING STORM

The policy of the Trust was to make criticisms with constructive suggestions. Two quotations from Annual Reports reflect attitudes. One is (1990): 'Change is often desirable, frequently necessary and always inevitable. For eight centuries there has been change, but never so rapidly as now.' The other is from an earlier report: 'To travel hopefully is to arrive and the true success is to labour.' In the light of events to come, it was certainly essential to have such a philosophy. The Chairmen of the Trustees who steered the boat through stormy waters in these years were Mrs E.V.W. Proudfoot, Mrs C.M. Wolfe, Mr Robert Murray and Mrs D.M.M. Morrison.

Mr Nash resigned after many years of faithful work as Honorary Secretary. Mr Richard McFarlane took his place as Secretary and Minutes Secretary. In 1991 the Trust's new headquarters at 4 Queens Gardens were opened, and Mrs Isabel Dominiak became the indispensable Administrative Assistant.

Developments

The Golf Museum, 1988

The Links Trust proposed to erect a golf museum across the road from the Royal and Ancient Clubhouse. There were also plans by the Council for a car park on the Bruce Embankment. The Trust opposed these plans on the grounds that it would be a loss of open public space and it would entail the erosion of views. Here is another very apt reflection from a Trust report: 'Views are intangible but they are of particular importance to the spirit of a place.' (*How very true this is.*) The Trustees thought that it might be necessary to press for the Links to become a preservation area. The car park at the Bruce Embankment was built, and became fee-paying.

The Supermarket

William Low applied to build a supermarket at Kinburn Park and Jacob's Ladder. The bonus attached to this was that they would put up, at their expense, a large underground car park (and the need for a car park was becoming urgent). Although the Trust did advocate an underground car park, the Trustees objected to the scale of the buildings and the intrusion into public parkland. The Council turned down the application.

The Visitor Centre at the Castle

The Trust made suggestions on some aspects of the size and design. The Centre was sited as low down as possible; it has proved to be an asset to tourism.

Car Park

In 1990, in spite of objections, the Petherum car park was built. It runs down the east side of the North Haugh and up to the Argyle street car parks, and now has a Park and Ride system in the summer months. It is very well landscaped; there is a lot of greenery, and it is far less intrusive than might have been expected – and is indispensable.

Golf Courses

There was 'talk of more golf courses round St Andrews.' The Trust commented 'such applications entail new building in the countryside'. (*Little did we know then what was to come.*)

The Links Trust Clubhouse

The plans for this were examined in 1991. There was 'a high level of unease about the building and its intentions'. Plans for a modified clubhouse were then submitted, but objections were raised as to the site and its effect on other local businesses (there was to be a retail outlet). It seemed essential to erect a clubhouse for the use of the public and visiting golfers who were not members of the existing clubs. Up to now the Links were almost free of buildings, apart from Pilmuir Cottage and the old shepherd's cottage at the third tee on the Eden, and also sheds for equipment. It was sad that the natural setting of sea and links, for centuries unbroken, had to be impinged on, but the Links Clubhouse is well designed and much used. The inevitable car park is a large blot on the green landscape.

Waiting in the Wings

There were plans by developers for housing schemes on the outskirts of St Andrews:

1. At Little Carron (west of the town).
2. At Balone Farm Steadings.
3. At Brownhills House for a group of Timeshares; this would entail cutting down a prominent group of pine trees. Objections were made and the application turned down.
4. For conversions and extensions at Feddinch Farm (permission granted).
5. Plans by Muir for a huge development on the south slopes between the Largo Road and the Anstruther Road which would increase the size of the town by one third. There was an outcry from the public, many objections, and a petition was submitted. The application for this scheme was withdrawn.
6. For building 99 residential units at St Nicholas Farm (East Sands).

There was a spreading unease about the general situation. I wrote of my own feelings:

Sitting in a cottage with its thick-built walls
I heard the tractor throttle brake and stop.
I watched the earth scooped up, set down,
displaced and dumped.
I heard the sullen thump and churn of mixers,
I watched the sky-high cranes manouevre and
precisely place each concrete block.
The buildings grew and halved my dome of sky.
Once you could see the scan of hills
and green fields sloping to the city's edge,
a compact site stitched in by links and sea.
For centuries the pilgrim roads approached
the towers, the spires, a city built in stone.
Mourn for what's been lost.
Insidiously gap breathing places plugged,
virgin sites attacked, carbuncles spawned,
views marred. But after shedding tears,
stand up and fight.

Final Draft of St Andrews Local Plan 1992

The Trust made objections to the local plan stressing that 'it is essential St Andrews is not allowed to spread beyond its present boundaries'. They submitted that there was need for traffic control, for control of the western approaches, for control in the harbour area. The Trust asked that 'the Harbour Trust remain in existence when the new unitary plan comes in'.

Public Inquiry into the St Andrews Local Plan

The Inquiry, which was chaired by Miss Janet McNair, dragged on for several weeks. Mr Sandy Bollard Q.C. put forward a submission on behalf of the Trust to the effect that St Andrews should be protected, and its present boundaries maintained. Again there was a request for St Andrews to have Green Belt status, and also to be nominated for a World Heritage site.

In 1995 the Inquiry Report on the Local Plan was published. It stated that no further development should take place in St Andrews until the Strategic Study and Traffic Plan by Fife Regional Council was completed. The Reporter accepted the Trust's contention that views into, as well as out of, St Andrews have considerable environmental importance. The Reporter also recommended restrictions on the size of the St Nicholas Farm development. In January 1996 the Council approved an amended plan for the St Nicholas development; this must go forward as there was a need to supply 'affordable housing'. The development was for 67 units only, the site being restricted to an area running less than halfway up the hill on the north side of the A917. From here there is a fine view of the medieval town. The plan ensured that the houses were built low down to make them less visually intrusive. In the sixties the University had already developed the area beyond the Gatty Marine by erecting a large group of unattractive flats for students.

A Stream of Submissions, 1996

Application was made to redevelop buildings on the west corner of Abbey Street and South Street for a Harry Ramsden Fish Restaurant. The Council turned this down in view of many letters of objections by the Trust and others. Parking problems were a major factor.

Byre Theatre

There was an application by the Byre Theatre Company to rebuild. A large model of the new building was put on display. It was to be of predominantly of glass, and much larger and higher than the previous building. The plans included the demolition of a house in Abbey Street. Objections were lodged by the Trust. Some adjustments were made, and the Council gave its consent.

There were considerable delays in the building programme, and with them increasing costs. These were met with an Arts Council grant which, by June 2001, amounted to a total of £4.15 million; Fife Council gave £625,000 and Scottish Enterprise Fife £249,500. Our own necessary contribution was raised locally. When completed, the Byre had cost £5.2 million.

The new Byre Theatre was opened by Sir Sean Connery on 5 June 2001. The interior of the building was a triumph for Nicoll Russell Studios and architect Scott Turpie who won the competition for the Best Small Theatre in Scotland. It has had a very successful year and is functioning as a busy community theatre and centre, open 10 a.m. to midnight.

St Leonards Fields

St Leonards School put this boarding house and its grounds on the market. The Trust had recommended it as a site for a new health centre and/or hospital in preference to a green field site. A developer put forward plans to acquire St Leonards Fields for a housing scheme. Miss Ruth Day represented the Trust at the Local Public Inquiry. The objections to the housing scheme were based on overdevelopment, inappropriate design and the possible use of the site for a health centre/hospital. The application was turned down. (Modified plans were later submitted and were passed in October 2000.)

Application for flats

The Trust made no objections to plans for the erection of flats at 52 Argyle Street, nor for Flats at 106-110 Market Street, but it was remarked that none of these would fulfil the needs of first-time buyers.

Extension Building for the Gatty Marine Laboratory; Erection on the North Haugh of a new Molecular Science Laboratory

It seems that the Trust had little say in these two developments by the University. Most people seem to have been unaware of the plans. The Gatty Marine has a worldwide reputation for its research, and the extension was to provide facilities for research on seals and other sea mammals. In size and shape this new building is intrusive in the landscape, especially when seen from the east entry to St Andrews. The East Sands have lost their charm. No longer do the sands run by farming land to the cliffs.

The Molecular Science Laboratory on the North Haugh came as a real shock, in shape size, colour and its weird surrealist roof appendages. The comment of the Trust was: 'the building was massive and obtrusive and not at all what was expected'. Here we find for the very first time in its sixty-two years a revealing comment: 'The Trust feels itself powerless to do anything'. No longer was the University co-operating with the Trust.

Pilmour Cottage

Plans by the Links Trust to demolish Pilmuir Cottage on the Links to make way for new Links Trust Offices were vehemently and successfully opposed by the Trust and others. Amended plans were submitted to include the cottage in the offices. The premises are now finished and functioning.

Council Changes

In April 1997 a change took place which was to affect St Andrews greatly. North East Fife Council with its headquarters at Cupar ceased to exist. The whole of Fife came under Fife Council with headquarters at Glenrothes. Some sub-departments still function at Cupar, but they are answerable to Fife Council. Our locally elected councillors are in a political minority in the event of a decision by the ruling Council. We have our St Andrews Community Council; it has a voice but no powers.

The Preservation Trust's Role

The work involved in scanning all the applications was time-consuming. Out of two hundred applications per annum the Trust made objections and suggestions to 20-25% of the planning applications submitted. About half resulted in the Council's refusal of the plans. The Trust had to pay fees for professional advice and representation, and its funds were low. When Mr Timothy Tynte-Irvine took over in 1993 as the Trust's Finance Convener, his aim was to put the Trust's finances on a sure footing; this he had successfully accomplished by the time of his retirement in 1999. Sadly he died soon after this and the Trust lost a good friend. Tony Hardie has continued to maintain the high standards involved in this arduous role.

The Battle for a Green Belt for St Andrews

It will be appreciated that, with the loss of the North East Fife District Council and with the filing of applications by the developers, St Andrews seemed to stand in danger of being swamped. After the 1982 public enquiry on the Draft Local Plan, the first recommendation of the Reporter was that 'developments to the west and south of the town should be severely restricted'. Our District Council corroborated this decision, but St Andrews now came under a planning committee for East Fife. In early 1997 the Preservation Trust commissioned David Tyldesley, eminent landscape architect, to make an advisory report on a green belt. Soon after this report had been studied and discussed, a meeting was called of local organisations. A committee was formed, and a Green Belt Forum was established, with Robert Murray as Chairman. Terry Lee succeeded as Chairman in 1998, with Elizabeth Williams (Convener of Planning to the Preservation Trust) Secretary. The Forum got down to its vital work at once. Before long, over thirty local and national organisations had joined.

The St Andrews Strategic Study

In March 1998, the Trust, the Forum and the public received copies of the St Andrews Strategic Study: The Consultation Report by Fife Council. The document was impressive; there was information, an invitation to the public to express their preferences on further development and sites. One option was no further development, as plans were already made for enough building to satisfy our area quota up to 2011. Of interest in the study was the fact that between 1991 and 1996 an average of 73 houses were built each year in the St Andrews area. The plans showed every danger of what was, in Green Belt terms, 'urban sprawl'.

Three statements were made in the section *Landscape Issues* in the report:

> (1) St Andrews is at its landscape capacity and no major expansion should take place. (2) The landscape setting of St Andrews is crucial to its character and must be protected and enhanced. (3) There is a need to contain the spread of the Town and a green belt must be seriously considered as a way of achieving this.

There was an exhibition and a period for public consultation. The Green Belt Forum led the way with publicity and with meetings, and there was a great response.

I will stay with the subject of the green belt and, for the moment, mention only the growing concern of the Preservation Trust at plans being submitted to the Council for large, golf-related developments to the south, the east and the west of the town. The Trust wrote to Mr Dewar (the Secretary of State) asking that these developments should be called in. The Forum also wrote to him, urging that a green belt should be considered 'as a mode of future control over development'. His officials decided that it was a matter of policy that such matters should be resolved locally.

On 28 January 1999 Fife Council held a meeting regarding the Written Statement on the Fife Structure Plan. The planners had decided that there was *no need for green belts in Fife*. And further, they stated that 'fewer of the characteristics required for Green Belt designation were exhibited at St Andrews than in Dunfermline and Glenrothes'. *The Citizen* headlined its report as 'SLAP IN THE FACE FOR TOWN GREEN BELT'.

The draft policy for the new Fife Structure Plan duly came out. *The Courier*'s headlines on 16 March 2000 were 'FIGHT INTENSIFIES IN BID FOR GREEN BELT'. The Green Belt Forum called a public meeting in the Town Hall. Professor Lee said, 'the draft flew in the face of the overwhelming view of people who responded to the Council's own St Andrews Strategic Policy. Mrs Williams said, 'The council appeared to have drawn up rules which did not tally with Scottish Office guide lines for a green belt.' The fight was on: the Green Belt Forum organised a Royal Mail drop of 10,000 leaflets urging people to send their objections in writing to Fife Council. There was a good reponse. It had its effect, and there were hopeful signs that there was a change of thinking.

The Strategic Plan 2001

When this was published, there was dismay. The flaws in the Plan are best described by Professor Lee who wrote as follows.

> We were grateful to be offered a Green Belt at all, but the Planners gave birth to a curiously deformed creature. It

> failed to conform to the national guidelines. It had a large and ominous gap in the south west. … We campaigned vigorously alongside the Preservation Trust for a more normal Green Belt. It is hard to think of an environment more suited to a continuous encircling belt allowing for foreseeable but controlled expansion.

The Forum sent a document to the Scottish Executive expressing its views on the Council's Strategic Plan.

On January 2002 all those who had supported the aims of the Green Belt Forum received by post from the Scottish Executive its detailed amendments to the Fife Structure Plan. *The Citizen*'s headlines over its report were 'THUMBS UP FOR THE GREEN BELT! Scottish Executive decision hailed as a victory for "people power"'. Professor Lee's comments on this were as follows:

> The review and decision by the Scottish Environmental Ministers is that the plan should be modified so that the Green Belt fully encircles the town. The report gives as an example the sort of boundaries set out by David Tyldesley – a landscape architect commissioned by the Trust in 1997.
>
> The usual exemptions for agricultural, recreational and forestry developments and such are referred to, but the modifications go even further. They apply to the principle of 'inter-visibility'. For instance there would be 'a presumption against development' of a new golf course if it could be seen from the town. …
>
> It must be seen as a rare tribute to the principal of consultation. It appears that representation by ordinary people can work.

He added the proviso that the Council had six weeks to defend its original proposals. It has since been confirmed that St Andrews has been given a Green Belt that encircles the town.

Departure Hearing, June 1999: Kingask, Scooniehill, Feddinch

This meeting was called because of a Departure from the Local Plans (referred to below). The most compact way to present the long saga of these three applications for golf courses and large auxiliary developments is by an account of this Departure Hearing. It was called to consider applications for:

1. Kingask (see below)

2. Scooniehill

Outline application by St Andrews International Golf Club Ltd. for a 500-acre site for two 18-hole golf courses, clubhouse, leisure facilities, residential units of 80 member's suites of a combination of one-, two- and three-bedroom suites, a golf academy.

The existing steadings at Scooniehill Farm would be demolished. The proposed buildings would be south and east of the steading, and would be clearly seen from the southern approaches to St Andrews. The site of 500 acres is between the St Andrews to Largo A914 and the Grange road; it extends to the south beyond the ridge of the hill. It is cropped or grassed and is grade 2 and 3 agricultural land; also it is designated as an area of Great Landscape Value. At the request of Council the applicants had made a traffic impact assessment, a landscape assessment, and a full supporting statement incorporating details of economic impact. Objections were lodged by the St Andrews Preservation Trust, the Community Council, and eight national associations. Clayton Hardisty spoke on the danger to children living at Wester Balrymonth Farm Steadings, sited on the proposed golf courses. (The application was later turned down by the Council, and subsequently the Company submitted amended plans. These were refused at a meeting of the East Area Development Committee in Cupar on 30 May 2000. The developers appealed; there was an Inquiry in November 2000, when the plans were turned down.)

3. Feddinch (to the west of the Scooniehill area)
Outline application for a Leisure Development including 18-hole golf course, 600 holiday units, 150/200-bedroom hotel, clubhouse and 350 conference suites, spa, sports leisure facilities and golf range at Lumbo Farm. Feddinch Estates and Mount Melville Estates in all cover 420 acres. The applicant, Mr M.A. Johnstone, was advised to submit detailed reports on various aspects. The plans were altered and resubmitted at the end of 2001. These plans consist of making two golf courses and a block of time-share flats. The trees screen the area, so the building and courses would not be seen from the town. The developers say the project would not be started (unlike Gateway) until the cost has been covered by subscribers.

So at 2 p.m. on 17 June 1999 we trooped into the Town Hall and filled the Council Chambers, to be present at the Strategic Development Committee Departure Hearing. The members of this Committee sat facing us. High on the walls hung the portraits of former Provosts. (*It seemed from their expressions they could hardly believe what was being discussed. Nor at times could some of us; the enormity of the proposed developments seemed like a nightmare.*)

We were given information sheets with the details of each development and the order of speakers. Only those who had made objections and had applied to speak were on the schedule; those representing bodies were allowed ten minutes, and individuals five minutes.

Only councillors might address questions to the Chairman. The booklet gave various relevant statements: appendix M gave the salient points of the January 1996 Landscape Character Assessment of St Andrews carried out by Mr David Tyldesley and commissioned jointly by Fife Regional Council, North East Fife District Council, and Scottish Natural

Heritage. A more detailed assessment of Fife's Landscape character also by Tyldesley had been considered by the Fife Strategic Committee on 28 June 1998. It was agreed that 'these will be a material consideration in the determination of planning applications'. One point in the report was that all of the landscape round the town was sensitive to development, but that some areas were more sensitive than others, particularly the areas to the south, parts of the south-west and the area along the coast.

There was an appendix on PAN 43, Planning Advice Notes by the Government On Golf Courses and Associated Developments. Some extracts follow. 'In view of the debates about a Green Belt for St Andrews PAN 43 suggests that green belts may in some cases be suitable locations for golf courses. However the PAN does caveat that suggestion with advice that golf courses using existing buildings or with little or no associated development are likely to cause the least impact'. 'Where a planning application includes a golf course and a related development, key issues for evaluation will be whether the golf course is of primary or secondary significance to the development.'

Kingask

The first of the three applications heard was that of Kingask, and I will deal with its story up to the present.

Kingask is just over two miles east of St Andrews on the north side of the A917 St Andrews to Crail road, stretching from Kingask farmhouse, and including Kinkell and up to Winchester; it runs from the road to the coast where it begins at the Rock and Spindle and ends beyond the Buddo Ness. The site covers 210 hectares (520 acres), most of it is classified as Grade A prime agricultural land. It is located within an Area of Great Landscape Value. The coastal area contains a site of Special Scientific interest; an iron Age fort lies within the area at Kittocks Den.

The story of 'the Kingask development' began doucely. In 1990 North East Fife Regional Council received from a local farmer an application for a development at Kingask. The plans were for an 18-hole good quality golf course for visitors; a clubhouse for 200-250 members; a second golf course for family and beginners; a 30-50 bedroom hotel (3 star); a small exclusive leisure area (sauna, pool, etc.); a range of bar and restaurant facilities in the hotel and clubhouse. The buildings were to be a combination of conversion and new buildings based on the existing farm steading and land to the west. Here is an extract: 'Attention will be given to the scale and character of new buildings so that they are fully integrated into their landscape setting. Conversion will respect the character of the existing buildings, and new buildings will reflect indigenous architecture.' There was only one objection. Outline consent was given on 13 June 1990. The re-use of the redundant traditional farm buildings and the building of a small-scale hotel in a discreet and secluded part of the site was a part of the original assessment and subsequent planning approval. There is a large group of screening trees at the farmhouse. No move was made to follow this up until 16 January 1998 when a renewal of outline consent with minor conditions was given to exactly the same proposal with all the same components. But this time the applicant was the St Andrews Bay Development Company of Dr Donald Panoz, a multi-millionaire and the owner of a very successful pharmaceutical business, ELAN, in Dublin. (He had taken out Irish citizenship before he set up Elan thirty years ago.) He owns the Diabolo Grandi in California, the Chateau ELAN golf complex in Georgia, the racing track Automotive at Le Mans and the Raceway Hotel in Florida.

It was an innocently seductive application; butter wouldn't melt in its mouth. In August 1998 the Council welcomed the American entrepreneur and his wife with open arms, gave a reception in their honour, and apparently fell under their spell. What happened between then and the bombshell in mid-October when the developers submitted a new set of plans is only rumour and guesswork. These plans by the St Andrews Bay Development Company were for:

1. A 240-bedroom hotel to be built on a site near the sea.
2. Conference facilities for 600.
3. A gatehouse facility.
4. 10 individual hotel accommodation buildings, described as 'Scottish Manors'(!), each comprising two units of 4 bedrooms (i.e. 80 bedrooms).
5. New access; internal road system and parking areas; landscaping.

There was a request for the inclusion of an additional piece of land to form an extension to the golf courses. The steadings site would now be used for an indoor golf centre, indoor clubrooms, outdoor tennis court, restaurant and bar retail units; maintenance sheds. An amazing statement says, 'The buildings were designed to read as a linked family of developments rather than individual unrelated buildings. Direct reference has been made to the Scottish Arts and Crafts movement and also to the work of Sir Robert Lorimer.' (We now know that the plans are a mirror image of Dr Panoz's Atlanta hotel.)

The application was turned down by the East Area Development Committee on 9 February 1999. Briefly, the reasons given were:

1. Visual amenity: the size and location would detrimentally affect a designated area of great landscape value and its proximity to the coast would have an adverse impact on views from the coast footpath.
2 In the interests of landscape amenity and to protect the quality of

the environment, the proposed development would result in the loss of existing landscape character, would not be appropriate to, nor in keeping with, its landscape setting, and would have an adverse effect on the landscape setting of St Andrews.

3 (summary) The development would result in significant additional movement of construction vehicles, sewerage tankers and other vehicles through St Andrews. This would add to existing traffic congestion. Significant additional traffic generated by the scheme would disturb the residential area of Lamond Drive.

The developers made an appeal on the refusal of planning permission which was lodged with the Secretary of State.

At a continuation of the Committee meeting, a slightly amended and larger overall plan was submitted. The following changes were made:

1. The hotel to have 208 bedrooms.
2. The Conference Centre to have a 400 maximum capacity.
3. The individual hotel accommodation buildings to be reduced to 40 bedrooms and to be relocated.
4. A much larger spa building, which had previously been marked for a future application, to be relocated to the steadings.

The following bodies made representations against the St Andrews Bay Co. plans (those starred gave oral submissions at the Hearing):

The St Andrews Preservation Trust*
The Royal Burgh of St Andrews Community Council*
The Scottish Civic Trust
The Architectural Heritage Society for Scotland
Royal Fine Art Commission for Scotland
Scottish Environment Protection Agency
St Andrews Green Belt Forum*

The Scottish Civic Trust
The St Andrews Merchants Association,
The Association for the Protection of Rural Scotland*
The Scottish Rights of Way Society*
Historic Scotland
Scottish Natural Heritage
eight individuals*

There had been 163 letters of objection and 60 letters of support. May I interject with regard to the letters of support for the Kingask, that paid canvassers visited houses and firms throughout Fife, and even in Edinburgh, with forms saying 'Sign here for jobs.' They got short shrift in some St Andrews shops; most shopkeepers do not think that large self-sufficient golf complexes bring customers to the town. There were some who were attracted by the 'Jobs Promised' aspect; there are 500 construction jobs – and without doubt some Fife contractors are benefiting from the Kingask construction work – but when the development is up and running there will be only 275 permanent jobs. In St Andrews there is a shortage of applicants for hotel jobs.

Apart from the developer's representative, one of the speakers was in favour of the Kingask plans, and all others were against. Dorothea Morrison, Chairman of the Preservation Trust, made objections for the following reasons:

1. The plans were a violation of Development Plan policies relating to the protection of the countryside and unbuilt coastline.
2. It was contrary to the findings of the Strategic Study. The Trust emphasised the findings of this Study, in particular the crucial importance to St Andrews of its setting, and the fact that green belt issues must be a material consideration in determining any planning applications.
3 Regarding tourism, there would be a negative impact from such a large building.

4. Location of the buildings: a clubhouse on the most prominent part of the site is totally unacceptable.
5. Traffic impact: these issues had not been realistically addressed.
6. Economic impact: the likelihood of satisfactory full-time employment for more than a few people is queried. Jobs would be mostly seasonal.
7. The Trust considers the amended proposal to be even larger than its predecessor and addresses none of the grounds given for the Council's refusal.

There follows a summary of other points made by written or oral submissions, in addition to those above given by the Trust which were substantiated in various ways.

- The plans are contrary the St Andrews Local Plan, and are against Council policy.
- The development would be visually intrusive by day and night. The lights from the hotel complex would be seen all along the Fife and Angus coasts. There would be a loss of prime agricultural land.
- No survey and analysis of the site for the golf courses, including its ecology, archaeology, and landscape history, have been submitted.
- Traffic: much had been made by the developers of using transport organised by the company to reduce the numbers of cars. The comments were: 'the hotel management cannot dictate how or when conference delegates will arrive at conferences. The traffic management plan has been based on assertions rather than numeric assessment of the traffic flows.' 'No need has been demonstrated for the countryside location of such a large hotel and leisure complex and conference centre in this sensitive location rather than in an urban settlement area.'
- 'The scale and bulk of the development is unacceptable within an Area of Great Landscape Value.'

Objections against the hotel were:

1. 'Density mass and effect on the landscape'.
2. Concern over quality of materials.
3. Standard of design and overall scale have not been considered in the new submission
4. The hotel design has been predicated by the design of another existing hotel complex in USA operated by the applicant (not based on Lorimer's designs!).
5. The proposed built development would not be compatible with criteria in national planning policy, guidance and current development plans to ensure appropriate and sensitive siting.

The Scottish Environment Protection Agency quoting Section 75: 'agreement is required to regulate the sewerage disposal pending the availability of the public sewer. (An estimated two lorries a week would have to transport sewerage through St Andrews for some months; it was commented that two a day would be more likely.)

Others made the points that the approval of Kingask would open the floodgates to further developers and that 'the scale of the Conference Centre is not leisure but an industry'.

Mr MacKinnon, agent for the developer spoke. He emphasised the money and jobs Kingask would bring; he dealt blithely with the traffic issue – the Transport Department had it all in hand. During the building process ten lorry movements a day were calculated and agreed on.

Somewhat dazedly we switched to the Scooniehill debate. There was a short adjournment at six o'clock. When we reassembled we heard that the applicants for the Feddinch development were withdrawing the plans for the time being.

Press reactions

Here are some extracts from Jim Crumley's column 'A Personal View' in *The Courier & Advertiser, 29 June 1999*:

GOVERNMENT HEALTH WARNING.

> What follows, if you happen to be involved in developing Kingask near St Andrews, or if you happen to be one of the members of Fife Council's area development committee meeting today to pronounce in the fate of Kingask, could put you off your breakfast, I hope.
>
> New readers can start here in a small town on the sea. At its core is a medieval survival of streets and proportions shadowed and shone by the hard light of east coast suns. ... Countless travellers from countless shores have washed up here and been grateful, moved beyond reason by an aura which seems to amount to more than the sum of its parts. People dream dreams here. Among the most recent travellers is an American. Dr Donald Panoz gazed down lovingly on the town from Kingask and gave voice to the thoughts of countless coast walkers before him.
>
> 'We have something very special here,' he said. These are almost certainly the only words he has uttered since he came here with which you and I would agree. Dr Panoz did not mean the vigour of the sea and the poleaxing light and the pungent smells of history and tradition stirred his mortal soul and wrought poetry there. His subtext was very different. It went something like this (I paraphrase now, for effect and with the bias which befits a hostile witness):
>
> 'If I trash this headland with a damn great hotel and all the other money-spinning leisure bric-a-brac nobody

> really needs and use golf as an excuse to get it all up and running by the 2000 Open, I can make me a sweet fortune, take the money and run back to where I came from. We have something very special here.' He never actually spoke these words, of course, apart from the last six, but that is what, it seems to me, Dr Panoz is saying. I think we have something very malodorous here.
>
> The scheme is quite unnecessary, the site appears to have been chosen to give maximum offence and intrusion, the modifications proposed in response to public outrage were an insult. But more insulting by far is that Fife Council had its head turned and let itself be seduced. How could that have happened? There are few things more squirm-making than the sight and sound of strangers brandishing mega-bucks, then mysteriously persuading councillors and council officials to allow them to make more megabucks at the expense of the people who elected the councillors and pay the officials. No wonder Dr Panoz thinks he has something very special here.

The article goes on to describe the nature of St Andrews. It concludes:

> It does not need a 200-bedroom hotel any more than it needs two golf courses and the apparently compulsory accessories of leisure industry junk. What it does need is protection. Protection for its medieval heartbeat which, among other things, means the slowing and quietening of traffic. No one believes the Kingask project will do anything for the town other than make the burden of traffic intolerable on medieval streets and buildings.
>
> Protection for the wholly complementary environments of townscape and landscape setting with a

rigorously enforced non-negotiable green belt. Kingask is not just a particularly thoughtless concept. Build it and nowhere is safe. Deny it and create the desired impulse for a green belt for sanctuary and enlightenment.

The Courier & Advertiser, 8 July 1999:

£50 MILLION GOLF SCHEME GETS THE GO-AHEAD

Plans for the highly controversial £50 million golf, leisure and hotel development at Kingask were yesterday given the go-ahead by members of Fife Council. After a lengthy discussion at a session of the authority's Strategic Development Committee the bitterly opposed but biggest ever investment to come to Fife was approved by 12 votes to five. The consent will be subject to strict planning conditions and a uniquely worded agreement aimed at imposing rigid controls on the traffic movements in and out of the Kingask site.

The only remaining issue to be settled comes in the form of outstanding demands from North-east Fife's MSP and MP, St Andrews Preservation Trust and the Community Council for the matter to be called-in by the First Minister, Donald Dewar, and subjected to a full public enquiry.

There were disappointed and sometimes angry comments from the wide array of national and conservation bodies and organisations who had put forward formidable opposition to the Kingask plans. Under the heading 'Fury at the Rape of St Andrews' there are comments from some of these bodies. A few extracts will suffice. 'The decision was not surprising, Dr Don Panoz had been paraded in front of the media.' 'Planners are now so American obsessed that Kingask is reported to have a prairie landscape. [This refers to 'The existing barren and prairie style landscape …', Birrell-Planning Report, 9.2.99.] Need we say more?' Dr Frank Riddell, Chairman of the St Andrews Community Council: 'It did not seem to have mattered that the Fife Structure Plan, the St Andrews Local Plan, the St Andrews Strategic Study, the St Andrews Traffic Strategy and the St Andrews Tourism Strategy argued strongly against development at Kingask. Their policies were abandoned and rejected in the committee papers prepared by the officials. They ignored the conclusions of the government's inspectors for Historic Scotland, and the government agency Scottish National Heritage. They selectively quoted from their own consultants' reports to arrive at the planning outcome they desired. The outrage felt by local people at the rape of our beautiful town is enormous. The people of St Andrews must rely on the goodwill of the First Minister to call in this application.

There was further trouble. Allegations made by Peter Douglas, Chairman of the East Area Development Committee, were published in the local paper. Peter Douglas is a retired Minister of the Church of Scotland with a high reputation. He claimed that council employees had told him that they were put under pressure 'to come into line or stay silent' in relation to two planning applications. (Later, when they might have greatly helped the cause, they were unwilling to have their names revealed; this may be understandable in view of their careers.) Fife's Chief Executive, Douglas Sinclair, asked John Anderson, former Chief Executive of Glasgow City Council, to investigate these allegations. He found that there was no evidence that officers had been put under pressure to 'trim their reports' or to 'Come into line and stay silent'. However, the report highlighted areas where improvements might be made and set out recommendations which were acted upon. Mr Anderson strongly criticised the Council regarding the actions of the Communications Unit.

Gavin Bell of *The Scotsman* wrote about the mixed reactions he found when discussing the matter with various people in St Andrews.

> There are those who regard the new tourist playground as an outrage, those who think it will be good for business, and as usual a lot of people who could not care less. There is no doubt that the increasing volume of traffic is a problem. Curiously the local golfing fraternity is not jumping for joy at the prospect of more playgrounds. The prevailing wisdom is that more courses mean more golfers, and extra pressure on the existing facilities which are struggling to meet demand. There are already six golf courses in the town including the Old Course, and another four miles away, and all of them are heavily subscribed. The odds on being selected from a daily ballot for a round on the Old Course in summer is currently seven to one.
>
> The choice of name 'St Andrews Bay Development Company' is significant. Kingask is scarcely thought of as St Andrews Bay, though from the hotel the bay may be seen, and accordingly the hotel from the bay. To international golfers the name St Andrews spells 'The Old Course'. Come to the Mecca, stroll out from your Kingask luxury hotel and have a round on the Old Course. But, surprise, surprise, it's not in with the deal. Set up a golf Disneyland with fifty million pounds and become a member of the R and A – surprise again, neither is that in the deal.

Bell interviewed Peter Mason of the Links Trust who said, 'Experience leads us to believe that any development encouraging golfers to come to St Andrews will increase demand for our facilities. In the recent past five new courses have opened within the area, there has been no diminution in the demand for play on our links. We can expect quite a few new arrivals to wander in this direction.' His tone suggests that Bell was not overjoyed.

The Kingask decision brought widespread publicity and criticism.

The developers moved on to the site immediately after the approval of the plans, and by February 2000 work was well under way. An article by Alan Taylor in *New Statesman Scotland*, 21 February, includes the following.

> St Andrews' problem lies in its relative isolation which in the past was a large part of its charm. It is bedevilled by the lack of a railway link, poor road access and limited car parking spaces. There is the problem of the Old Course itself, which is the prime reason why so many make the pilgrimage to this blasted heath. Imagine, for example, Catholics arriving in Rome to be told that St Peters was out of bounds. Some 42,000 rounds can be played on the Old Course annually, which means that many people arrive in hope and return in disappointment.

He ends the article: 'In such circumstances the historical, hallowed role of St Andrews is up for exploitation. And nor can it have much cause for complaint. [Fife Council] having sold itself to the devil, it had little option but to live with the consequences.'

Who would contest the decision to give the Kingask go-ahead? At its meetings in September and November 1998. The St Andrews Community Council discussed the Kingask development and decided to oppose the plans and to take any further action deemed appropriate. This was endorsed at its meeting in January 1999 by 9 votes to 2, with 3 abstentions. The Community Council with the support of the MP the MSP and a variety of national and local bodies appealed to the First Minister that the Kingask and other related developments at Scooniehill and Feddinch should be 'called in'. A letter dated 23 July from the First Minister's office declined the request for a call-in.

A special meeting of the St Andrews Community Council was

called for 2 August 1999 at the request of concerned members of the public who had already raised £10,000 to meet the legal costs of a fight. The Chairman opened the meeting thus:

> This meeting has been convened at the request of 200 members of the public, who appear to be electors in St Andrews. ... We are requested to consider counsel's opinion concerning the decision taken by Fife Council as regards the Kingask development and to take any further action we deem appropriate.

Cupar solicitors Bennetts had been approached independently to obtain Counsel's opinion on the validity of the Kingask decision. Mr Bennett's clients intended to present counsel's opinion for the Community Council to consider any action that might be possible according to the terms of the opinion. The most likely action would be a call for a judicial review on the subject. The Chairman was invited by Mr Bennett to attend a private meeting with senior counsel in Edinburgh on 23 July. Two other local representatives and Mr Bennett were present at this meeting. Quoting from the Chairman's introductory remarks at the meeting:

> I defined these aims as halting the Kingask development either permanently, or for a minimum period of around six months. I also made it clear that I believed that the Community Council would only act if counsel's opinion were sufficiently strong and that there was a sufficient finance available to the Council to cover all eventualities.
>
> *A meeting of this type is unprecedented for the Community Council and poses special problems for all members. For a Community Council to consider the possibility of launching legal action against its parent body*

> *is an exceedingly grave step and should be taken only after the best possible advice has been obtained and then only after the most thorough consultation and discussion.* Accordingly the Chairman in consultation with the Secretary has invited certain people to be present at this meeting in order to obtain their advice and assistance as necessary. These people include Mr Bennett, Mr M. Campbell MP, Mr I. Smith MSP, Mr J. Purvis MEP, Cllr Rev. P Douglas (Chairman of the East Area Planning Committee), Mrs D. Morrison (Chairman, the Preservation Trust) and members of the public who funded the counsel's opinion.

The public was warned that because matters of a confidential nature would be discussed, at a certain point it would be necessary that the public be excluded, apart from those specially invited to the meeting. Sadly, the outcome was that the Community Council decided at a subsequent meeting on 3 August that it must drop the legal challenge. The meeting took two hours; the Chairman advised on the potential financial implications of taking legal action through the Court of Session and the possibility that the Community Council might not win their fight. 'Although there were statable grounds for raising proceedings against Fife Council for its handling of the Kingask affair, the Community Council will be best advised not to launch an action for a judicial review.'

Meantime the developers were getting on with the work. But things were not going as agreed. The section 75 traffic plan hammered out between Fife Council and the developers was said to be 'water-tight'. The number of ten lorries a day had been set, and there would be a strict check. The routes these lorries must take were clearly laid down. The Council would not hesitate to take the developers to court if the conditions were breached. It soon became apparent that this was being disregarded. At meetings of the Community Councils in the area, concern was expressed that the number of lorries using the site was exceeding the ten daily HGV trips allowed. Residents in the area around Peat Inn claimed the monitoring was very slack and was at first 'completely non-existent'. On 24 January 2000 the Fife Strategic Committee was told that the company had exceeded vehicle numbers, had been using unauthorised routes for HGVs, had damaged a minor road, and had breached a legal agreement. There was a discussion which resulted in a group vote by the dominant labour members. It was agreed that the lorry numbers could be doubled to twenty, that narrow country roads could now be used, and that the developers would pay the cost for damage already estimated at £35,000.

In *The Courier & Advertiser* of 26 January 2000 Mr Menzies Campbell asked how it could be possible for a section 75 agreement which the public had been assured had been fully negotiated was now 'found to be defective'. He asked various questions on how this had arisen.

To what extent do such matters rest on politics? I quote from a letter in *The St Andrews Citizen* on 4 February 2000. This was from Cllr Peter Grant (Glenrothes), a member of the Fife Strategic Committee. He describes the above meeting of 24 January: 'Among the petty abuse from Labour councillors who were determined to let the developer get away with it this time, we got an assurance from one that no party whip had been applied to the original application.' (This refers to the meeting of 7 August 1999 when planning permission was given.) 'I wonder why he felt he had to keep telling us that? I wonder if he had forgotten that at least two labour councillors turned up with their speeches ready written in support? I wonder if it was coincidence that one Labour councillor left the meeting as soon as the "let them get away with it" vote was taken, having stayed just long enough to give a Labour majority on the vital vote? But most of all I wonder how long it will take Fife Council to restore public confidence in its planning system.'

On 11 February there was a meeting of the Fife Strategic

Committee. The meeting was told that a survey carried out on one day in February had revealed 104 lorries using the site entrance (60 in and 44 out) and 83 using Lamond Drive (35 in and 48 out). On two other days members of the local community had monitored 46 heavy lorries going in to the site on the Tuesday, and 54 on the Wednesday. Anger was expressed and demands made for speedy action. Headlines appeared in the papers: 'COUNCIL MAY TAKE ACTION ON KINGASK'.

In an interview Mr Campbell said that the attitude of the developers in the face of local opinion was 'simply astonishing'. He said,

> Evidence was available that in their determination to proceed the developers were willing not so much to drive a coach and horses through the agreement but to drive as many lorries as they pleased. Protestations by Fife Council have a hollow ring in view of the undue enthusiasm which was shown for this project right from the very beginning. Those who were anxious that this development should proceed will no doubt be reflecting on how their trust has been abused.

As Mr Campbell foresaw, the Council decided not to take action. In discussion, agreement was reached with the developers: up to 35 heavy goods vehicles a day would be allowed to access the site until the end of June, with up to 20 one-way trips along the residential Lamond Drive. The decision was heavily criticised. One councillor, when interviewed by *The Courier & Advertiser* said that 'Fife Council appeared to be willing to roll over, put its paws up, and allow the developers to do exactly what they want.'

There is no need to say more on this subject. While all this was going on, somebody had taken action. There was to be a Judicial Review on Fife Council's handling of the Kingask development.

Continuous Business of the Trust

It is difficult to keep the time sequence, and there was a gap of five months before the Review took place. So I will now catch up with other activities, and go further, to update to 2002.

During the on-running development disputes, the business of the various committees of The Trust continued. The Planning Committee gave substantial support to the survival of the Woollen Mill building which had been sold to the Royal and Ancient Golf Club. The proposal to demolish what had been the first golf club factory in Scotland was vigorously opposed, and new plans were submitted which kept the original west face and the lines of the north frontage. The transformation of the old building was completed by the end of 2001 and is very acceptable.

Other plans submitted were for the 'Gateway Centre', on the north-east edge of the North Haugh, and the Trust made criticisms of certain aspects. The project was for a private golf club for businessmen; in return for the site, the company agreed to allow the University to have the ground floor as a University of St Andrews Museum. However, when the building was almost complete – at a cost of about £9 million – the company was forced to go into liquidation. It seems that no acceptable offer has yet been made.

The Trust Planning Committee put forward strong protests to plans by the University for a Brain Research Facility. While the proposed building was well designed, the idea of a modern building in the medieval garden of St Johns was completely unacceptable. The students agreed with the views of the Trust and protested vigorously, and the plans were withdrawn. The University had sold one of its smaller residences, Hepburn Hall in Kennedy Gardens. The development company had plans to change the house into flats, and to demolish and rebuild a block of student flats behind and to the south of the house. The Trust objected successfully to the size and the height of these flats, on the grounds that they would have a detrimental effect on the Lade Braes, and were not in keeping with the Hepburn Garden surroundings. Reduced plans were submitted and approved by the Council. Further applications of plans for a hotel complex at Kinkell, and for a similar development by the coast road near Kincaple were opposed, and both were refused planning permission.

In 2001 previous small committees were amalgamated to become the Publications, Publicity, Events and Membership Committee, with convener Mr K. Roberts. Mr Roberts designed two Christmas cards, which, together with a pack of notelets he designed from Trust paintings and photographs, have increased income. *The Citizen* and *The Courier* have continued to publish news of the Trust's activities, and photographs from the Trust's collection feature each week in *The Citizen.*

The Environment Committee has continued negotiations with the Council about the state of the Lade Braes. It also continues to tend the Trust's wood at Lawpark and to see to repairs on the doocots at Bogward and Kenley Green.

In 2001-2002 Elizabeth Thomas was convener of the Planning Committee; 156 applications were considered. Many of these involved extensive discussion and careful evaluation, and some necessitated site visits. Comments were submitted on ten applications, and objections were made to 36. Unfortunately, the objections to the extension to the Students' Union were unavailing. The Trust was not successful in its objections to the University's plan for a piecemeal demolition of the buildings comprising the David Russell Hall. These are to be gradually replaced by a Wester Langlands Student Village which will give an increase in residential accommodation. This increase is essential, and is part of the current policy of the University and its principal, Dr Brian Lang.

As a result of a campaign organised by Ken Roberts, who designed a full colour brochure entitled *St Andrews – A Future Worth Safeguarding*, 150 new members were recruited, bringing membership to about 1,000. Altogether, the Chairman's report for 2001-2 shows the Trust to be in a healthy state.

Impressions of the Judicial Review

There were a few courageous and public-spirited people who were not prepared to accept the way Fife Council had handled the Kingask affair. On 4 August 1999, the day after the Community Council's decision not to take action, Miss Penelope Uprichard went to her solicitor and asked if he could get another opinion. With five other petitioners she confirmed shortly that it was their intention to proceed.

It was necessary to raise enough money to cover the costs of a judicial review. The Review Funding Association was formed gradually over the next couple of weeks. Mr P.A. Hardie, Treasurer of the Preservation Trust, offered to take on the job of Treasurer to this (quite separate) Association. This is the timing of their programme; it proved to be an important factor.

6-13 Aug Collection of papers and reports, and study of case by the solicitor.
14 Aug Beginning of fund-raising.
19 Aug Memorial sent out by special courier to Senior Counsel.
27 Aug Senior Counsel said he was unable to take case, was going on holiday.
1 Sept Memorial sent to Lord Mackay of Drumadoon who accepted the case.
17 Sept Opinion received from Lord Mackay
18 Sept to 15 Oct The essential fund-raising continued.
16 Oct Junior Counsel drafted Petition.
18 Oct £28,300 having been raised, 1000 copies of a fund-raising letter were sent out.
22 Oct Mr MacKinnon, agent for the St Andrews Bay Development Company, was quoted on the front page of *The Citizen* as saying that St Andrews Bay could sue the Fund Raising Association and its supporters for millions.

(This was untrue, but it was the week after the papers had been filled with the result of the Hamilton-Fayed case, and it was much publicised that some of Hamilton's supporters would be liable to pay a proportion of the costs beyond that which they had pledged. However, that condition applies only under English law in libel cases. A letter submitted to *The Citizen* giving the correct legal position was published, but with the vital point omitted. This was rectified the following week, but it is likely that the error adversely affected the fund-raising. Throughout the Judicial Review, although reports appeared in other papers and regularly in *The Courier and Advertiser*, *The Citizen* did not report the progress of this local, unique and important case, but did present a large feature on a visit to Kingask by Dr and Mrs Panoz. The fund-raising went well and the group had the support of many St Andreans and other lovers of St Andrews living elsewhere.)

10 Nov	Consultation with Counsel.
18 Nov	Instructions given to Messengers-at-Arms to serve petition. They did not.
22 Nov	Petition for Judicial Review served. £50,000 had been raised (about half the estimated cost of the case; the final total of donations and pledges came to nearly £90,000).

The six petitioners (the Judicial Review Group) were Miss Penelope Uprichard, Mrs M. Sheila Adam, Mrs E. June Baxter, Ms Deborah Moffatt, Professor Terence R. Lee and Mrs Sheila M. Scott. The case was entered as Miss Penelope Uprichard and others against Fife Council and St Andrews Bay Development Company. Counsel for the Petitioners was Lord Mackay of Drumadoon, Q.C.; For the First Respondents (Fife Council): Gordon Reid, Q.C.; For the St Andrews Bay Development Company: Roy Martin, Q.C. The Hearings were on 12 and 13 January, then 27 and 28 January and 7 and 10 March 2000.

I went to the last two days of the Judicial Hearing; I had never before been present at a court case. My expectations were of something akin to scenes from a film or play, or from dramatic cases reported in newspapers. Nothing could have been further from the actuality. It was exciting being in the old Parliament House, walking through the corridors and Parliament Hall with its open timber roof, its portraits of famous men, and its great window depicting the inauguration of the Court of Session by James V in 1532. Books and papers were stacked on every available surface. There was a great bustle in this concourse, with black-robed men and women of the law, some wearing the impressive wigs of counsel, and their acolytes, all striding about looking very purposeful.

We found the court-room allotted to the hearing, where the public benches were almost filled. When Lord Bonomy made his entry – and throughout the proceedings – we were all impressed by the courtesy and the small ceremonies. It was amazing how civilised it was. There was no sign of strong emotions, antagonism or high drama. I thought at one point, when the meaning of a word was being discussed, that it was rather like a linguistics seminar at university. Lord Bonomy was a fatherly figure, relaxed and benign. Some of the exchanges between him and Lord Mackay might have been taking place in an interesting, laid-back discussion at a dinner party. He was genial, polite and very occasionally rebutted some point authoritatively.

There is no way in which a layman might have made a report on the six-day proceedings. Even if one could follow the main contentions, to understand it all one would have needed copies of the main references to precedents in relevant cases. But I will now give a brief informal outline of some of the events and impressions of the case. Those who are interested will find a fuller account in Appendix II which is based on the Judicial Report compiled by Lord Bonomy and received by Miss Uprichard three weeks after the case ended.

Lord Mackay spoke for the first day and a half; the principal submissions he put forward for the petitioners were: (l) that Fife Council erred in law by not requiring the developers to provide an environmental statement under Scottish Environmental Regulations 1988; (2) that the

Council failed to comply with their duties in not considering whether the development was a significant departure from the approved structure plan. Mr Reid for the Council was on his feet for much of the next three days. He dropped a bombshell on the third morning when he asked Lord Bonomy, before further proceedings, to rule on two points. The first was that the petitioners lacked title and interest to bring the case; this he based in the fact that none of them lived within the legal definition of 'neighbours' (to the site). The second was on the grounds of Delay (mora), that the petition was made nineteen weeks after their application was determined. Lord Bonomy gave his decision after lunch. With enormous relief we heard his ruling; he was satisfied that the petitioners were entitled to bring the proceedings. He would continue to hear the case of Delay and give his judgment in his report. The submissions on Delay went on for some time. One point made by Mr Martin was that the petitioners had failed to seek an interdict, and the cost of the work on the site now amounted to over £2.5 million.

Lord Mackay dealt with the failure of the Council to make an environmental assessment; when it came to Mr Reid being questioned about exactly when and by whom the decision *not* to have one was made, the Council met with some flak. Mr Reid had to admit there was no record. Lord Bonomy suggested that Mr Reid was 'presenting the situation as if it had simply evolved'. Mr Reid's defence rested on the ruling in a case made in 1915, that power to act on behalf of an authority may be delegated. There was a small exchange, which for a moment lightened things up. The case was by Dalziel School Board, against the Scottish Education Department. Lord Bonomy said he had to declare an interest as he had been a pupil at this school. 'I'm sorry my Lord', said Mr Reid, 'how was I to know?' He followed this with a remark that 'his Lordship is not that old anyway'.

Lord Mackay countered this by quoting two reports, the Tyldesley report and that of Scottish Natural Heritage. He concluded that the decision not to have an environmental statement was one that no planning authority, or official with or delegated power, would reasonably have made. The decision not to have one 'flew in the face of reason and was irrational'. Mr Reid seized on this and contended that if an issue is debatable or there is room for differing views, then irrationality cannot be established.

It was relevant, it was clever. But my mind kept going back to what was going on near St Andrews – to reality. I remembered one evening just after the Kingask development began. We were at our weekly poetry workshop. The day before, we had news of the start of the development. Workmen had demolished the long established beech hedge by the roadside and felled the treese. One member of the class read a poem she had written, expressing the feelings of all the people who cared deeply.

Kingask

Do you have any idea how angry we are,
How it hurts us to see what you are doing?
You have slaughtered the hedgerows,
the trees, wounded the fields.
Bandaging the gashes in smooth swathes of golf turf
will not heal the countryside.
And we weep
in helpless rage, in dismay.
Holy pilgrims travelled here
to these spiritual places
honoured them and loved them
(as we do) centuries ago
but you have assaulted them, mindless.
Will the spirit move away?
We hope it will not vanish,
trickle deep into bedrock, depart
on the winds for ever. But the skylarks
are silenced, orchids, primroses trampled
and we mourn for them.

Julia Prescott

Here are a few impressions from some of the six petitioners: 'Physically the experience was gruelling – getting up early, travelling on crowded trains, and sitting long hours on the most uncomfortable benches in the world in the overheated, airless court rooms'. The public benches are at the back, so that one sees, apart from the Judge, only the back of each speaker. It was difficult to interpret the way things were going. Sometimes it was not possible to hear Mr Reid, who spoke fast and in a rather soft voice: he often leaned forward and gazed earnestly at Lord Bonomy. Lord Mackay was impressive and made his points with clarity. There was certainly no high drama, but 'when a point was made or a point refuted there was a ripple of response'. Each of us paid close attention to Lord Bonomy and watched his reactions. He listened with intent interest; he made notes, he looked up cases which were referred to in the stacks of documents and books at his side and fed to him. Occasionally he asked a questioner for further clarification. Other impressions of him were 'he struck me as acute, with a superb memory, and a talent for finding anything he wanted in his notes at a moment's notice'. In between the days of this hearing he was sitting in judgment at other cases in other courts.

There were some lighter moments. At one point the court assistant lent a book to the Fife legal team, and Lord Bonomy had to ask for the book to be returned. His remark to the effect that perhaps Fife Council could not afford to buy their own books 'brought quiet hilarity' as did other exchanges. Another time Mr Reid said, 'The test which His Lordship adopts is really quite clear' and Lord Bonomy, with a wry smile, countered with the two words 'Is it?' Then again, Mr Reid said, 'The petitioners could have applied for a Judicial Review before the decision.' Lord Bonomy said that they did not know then that planning permission would be given. On one occasion Mr Reid was questioned on some documents concerning the decision by the Council not to require an environmental assessment. These were not available. Lord Bonomy smiled and said that it was a strange thing how often in his career he had heard that minutes of critical meetings were missing.

There was a good deal of discussion about golf courses and farming land. Lord Bonomy remarked that he had always considered golf courses as places of tranquillity. Mr Reid's rejoinder was, 'If that is so, your Lordship's golf must be better than mine'. Mr Rae, the Head of Planning Fife Council, and the Head of the Council's legal department constantly conferred as questions arose. At one point Lord Bonomy asked Mr Reid a question and followed this by saying he did not know what to think as half of the Fife team was nodding the answer 'yes' while the other half were shaking their heads 'no'!

Each day at the midday break the St Andrews group went for a light lunch in the café in St Giles Cathedral. (One of the group remarked that the cloakrooms in Parliament House were museum pieces, but there was up-to-date provision in old St Giles!) It was helpful to comment on and discuss matters at lunchtime and in the train going home. There were moments in court when it was very frustrating not to be able to contribute to the discussion, especially when a valid point on our side did not seem to be understood. Most of the time the members of the group were hopeful; they knew they had a good case. They found some of the passages fascinating; it meant so very much to the participants.

It was a relief when the hearing came to an end; the longer it continued, the higher the expenses would be for whichever side lost. Things might go either way – the petitioners did seem to have some cause for hope. But what if they did win? The building was so far advanced that the compensation would be enormous.

Lord Bonomy's report came to Miss Uprichard three weeks later, on 31 March 2000, and later the costs were settled. Her press release and letter to the papers made clear the outcome.

Kingask: post judgment press release, 31/3/00

What the petitioners set out to do was firstly to show that as objectors to the application for planning permission they had the right to bring the decision under review in the courts without having to be immediate neighbours. In this they succeeded. Their second aim was to show that the Council has breached the legal framework within which it has to work when handling planning applications of this sort. In this they have been unsuccessful, but not without Lord Bonomy expressing strong criticism of the way in which the Council recorded internal decisions on environmental impact and noting that it is not clear what the Council decided about Kingask in relation to the development plan.

The petitioners have also, of course, fervently wished to see this whole project halted because of the irreparable harm it will do to the character of this ancient town. It is a matter of profound regret to them and their many local supporters that this is now not to be.

The argument about delay is fully understood, and it was a risk that the petitioners took. Challenging the Council's decision without the benefit of legal aid was a massive task, however, for private individuals to undertake and the leading members of the Review Funding Association deserve praise for the energetic way they pursued the case, with the result that hundreds of public-spirited local residents have been willing to put their money where their mouths are.

It was feared from the day when local government reorganisation was announced that a Labour council based in Glenrothes would have a one-track mind on jobs when considering major planning applications from the St Andrews area. This fear has now proved to be amply justified, even though many of the jobs will only be short-term.

The Council should pay more attention to the wishes of the local community as expressed through their elected councillors and community council. The Council in Glenrothes has disregarded local democracy shamefully.

The Petitioners and their supporters hope that the Council in Glenrothes will, in the light of all that has happened, now think very carefully before again assuming the role of barbarians at the gates of St Andrews by ramming through any more such projects.

Following the later Hearing by Lord Bonomy regarding expenses, I quote from Miss Uprichard's letter to *The Citizen* on 2 June 2000. (The letter was in reply to a news item in *The Citizen* the previous week.)

With reference to your mention of a 'five months time lapse', the delay was not five months but three and a half months (the Judge agreed that it was not possible to present a petition until after the Community Council had made a decision on the matter).

Mr Harry Tait of the Fife Council's legal services stated that 'the petitioners had achieved nothing.' Mr Tait is mistaken. The Petitioners won on 'title and interest', which means the next petitioners to bring such a case will find their path easier. They lost on 'delay' because of the need to fund raise. The fact that their cause brought in £88,000 demonstrates the support throughout St Andrews and Fife, and further afield.

Because of the case the news of this battle spread far

and wide; there are frequent references to Kingask in current planning articles. In a recent article in a National newspaper (May 20th) reference was made to a planning débacle over a £50 million golf and conference centre development planned for Kingask.

The Petitioners lost the case. They were not, however, the subject of such comments from the court as were directed against Fife Council. The Judge was unhappy with the role of the local authority in this matter.

After consideration, he decided that justice would be done by awarding them only 50 per cent of their costs. The Judge said that he was departing from the usual rule that 'Expenses followed success'.

He also said that the Council had pointedly failed to say that it was an assessment of the likely impact on the environment that led to the decision that a statutory environmental statement was not required. It had been stated by the Council's legal representative that the decision had not been recorded anywhere …

The Judge when reviewing matters which there had not been time to hear fully in court said that he would have agreed with the petitioners that the Council had not given adequate reasons for granting the application. … they had not stated clearly what their position was in relation to the development plan. The relevant paragraph in the petitioner's petition with which he was agreeing begins 'that further and in any event the first respondents (Fife Council) acted in a procedurally unfair manner in granting the application'.

It should be remembered that this development was imposed on St Andrews having been turned down twice by the East Area Development Committee before it was called in to Glenrothes and approved by the Strategic

> Development Committee. On the evidence I would say that Mr Bill Brand's recent comment, that 'the Court's decision showed that the planning decision was sound' is at variance with the facts.

I have given a good deal of space here and in the Appendix to this unique and perhaps pivotal case. The Preservation Trust contributed a good sum to the fund.

CONCLUSION

When a book is completed, a line must be drawn with THE END beneath it. But of course there is no ending to the story of change in our much-loved St Andrews. The Founders and the Trustees of the Preservation Trust must have always been aware that change is inevitable – by decay, by demolition of buildings, by building and rebuilding, by roadworks. At the start, the Trust had the co-operation of the St Andrews Council with its planning powers (a rare concession), of the University and of the group of sympathetic local architects. But through the second half of the twentieth century, difficulties increased.

At the beginning of that century, St Andrews was a small place with a long history. The population was 9,600. The Kinnessburn was the boundary to the south; the building of handsome houses was taking place to the west. There was a clear distinction between the social classes which seems to have lasted longer here than in many places – into the 1960s. There was a 'County Set', and at that time *The Citizen* still printed under 'Hunt Ball' (or such occasions) the host and hostess, the name of their house and the list of guests in their party. The descriptions of weddings of the 'Upper Classes' included a full list of the presents and donors, and what dresses were 'favoured'. There have been welcome changes.

Of course, this was common to many places. One difference about St Andrews was that it never had any industry, other than fishing at sea, which ended mid-century, and the manufacture of golf clubs and golf balls, which was declining by the 1960s. Over the years we had a fresh stream of academics and their families, who, in the first seventy years of the century, had more leisure than they now have. St Andrews, being a small seaside town and the 'Home of Golf', and, moreover, enjoying more sun than the western part of Scotland, brought many people to live here in retirement. They had time to spare – consider what the Boase families and other public-spirited citizens did for St Andrews. The schools – St Leonards, Madras College and smaller private schools – and the University have given St Andrews a reputation for good education. Between 1957 and 1974, four new schools were built here: Madras Kilrymont (so that Madras became a Junior High and a Senior High), and the primary schools Langlands, Canongate and Lawhead Road. This indicates the growing population, the spreading of the town boundaries. The population (excluding students) was 9,457 by 1951, 11,480 by 1971, and 14,599 by 1991. The 2001 census figures will not be available until August 2002; at a guess the figure might be 18,000.

Changes are inevitable; the one which has made perhaps the biggest difference to St Andrews is the recent rapid expansion of the University and, consequently, the decrease in the ratio of number of townspeople to students. The aim, until the University acquired the North Haugh, was to make it 'a small residential university of excellence'. Student figures increased gradually from 1,678 by 1959 to 1,797 by 1979, and then rose sharply in the next two decades to reach 6,500 in 2001. By comparison with others, this University is small, and it has continued to grow in excellence, as shown by the high rankings in research, teaching, low drop-out rate and the success of graduates in finding work. However, it is no longer 'residential'. A large number of students have to live in houses and flats rented from absentee landlords. This has pushed up prices, made it difficult for incomers to buy homes, and also brought more development in the town centre, so that every small space is crammed with new flats. Relations between Town and Gown have suffered, as some of the students keep late hours, and inevitably disturb their neighbours. On the other hand there are considerable assets. The University brings to the town £77 million and provides 2358 jobs.

The traffic increases yearly and threatens the historic core of the town. The latest situation is that the Green Belt boundaries are not yet defined and there is further pressure from developers; one application covers 223 hectares on the south west, with two golf courses and one thousand houses!

As it has done since the Picts settled here, the sea tides ebb and flow. The students come and the streets are lively and cheerful; they depart and there is sense of loss. And always when out walking, one feels the pervading sense of history.

The Streets of St Andrews

Early Sabbath morn.
Pavements lighten, cobbles glisten,
spaces open, warmed by the sun.
A time to reflect.

We are the ancient ways
trodden by a thousand thousand feet
down the curfew-tolled days
of a millenium.

We have borne the weight and rumble
of carts, of coaches, carriages,
and now we know the ravages
of twentieth century traffic
a never-ceasing slick of tyres,
lurching double deckers, judder
of articulated lorries.

Better to think back
on the gentler imprints of bare feet,
sandals, wellies, paddle of galoshes,
trudge of seaboots, clatter of clogs,
firm tread of brogues.

Fashions we have known.
Daintiness of satin slippers,
naughtiness of dancing pumps,
swift pirouette of ballerina.
Court shoes, matronly. Painful stabs
of stilettos, prick of winkle pickers,
shuffle of baffies.

Roller skates, roller blades, skate boards
and wheels of prams where babies
dream their milky dreams, or regally
survey the scene.

The break is over,
the students once more here.
The joyful 'HI's ring out
and Big Hugs block the way,
Trainers and clump-heels meet,
stand, chat, stride cheerfully
into future years.

BW

Appendix I

BUILDINGS LISTED BY STREET, WITH ARCHITECTS

Number	Name	Architect	Date	Commissioned by
Hepburn Gardens South side				
14-16*		Gillespie & Scott	1906	
18-20*		Gillespie & Scott	1908	
22-24*		Gillespie & Scott	1910	
	*large double villas			
26	St Leonard's Church Manse	Gillespie & Scott	1905	
36		David Henry	1903-4	James Anderson
46-48		R. H. Motion		
50-52		A. Haxton & W. Walker (Leven)	1911	
	Newmill	Gillespie & Scott	1908	
	The Ridge (now Hepburn Hall)	Gillespie & Scott	1913	
92		Mills & Shepherd	1904	
96	Wayside	Sir Robert Lorimer	1901	
	New Park School		1860s	
102	West House	Mills & Shepherd	1906	
	Balnacarron		c.1900	
North side				
1	Thorncroft	David Henry (att.)	1880	
	Tullis House	Gillespie & Scott	1895	
5	Mucross	Gillespie & Scott	1897	
7	Strathaven	Gillespie & Scott	1897	
9	Rokeby	Gillespie & Scott	1894	
11	St Ronans	Gillespie & Scott	1894	
13	Estherville (now Rathairne)	David Henry (att.)	1895	for himself
15	Roseville	David Henry (att.)	1895	

Number	Name	Architect	Date	Commissioned by
17		Gillespie & Scott	1895	
21-23		Gillespie & Scott	1903	
33 & 35		David Henry	1907	
37 & 39		David Henry	1901	Bailie Scott
41 & 43		David Henry	1903-4	The Misses Thomson
61-67 (terrace)		Gillespie & Scott	1900	
Kennedy Gardens				
1	Argyle Lodge	Gillespie & Scott	1891	
2	Westlands	John Milne (att.)	1869-70	
3	Morlich	John Milne (att.)	1869-70	
4	Belmont	Jesse Hall	1867	A. Watson
	Rathelpie (The Free Church Manse)	John Milne (att.)	1856-57	
	Rathelpie Villa (now Rathmore)	John Milne	1861	Andrew Aikman
	Kinnessburn	George Rae	1863	
	Afton		1862	
	Liscombe	Thomas Cappon	1893-4	
	Westerlee (now Wardlaw Hall of Residence)	John Milne	1865-7	R. E Curwen
Wardlaw Gardens				
	Weston (now Hardens)	Jesse Hall	1867-8	
	Westgate	Jesse Hall	1867-8	
	Glenelg	David Henry (att.)	1880	
	Southgate	David Henry (att.)	1880	
Donaldson Gardens				
	Milford Lodge	Gillespie & Scott	1900	
	Wilberlea	Gillespie & Scott	1897	
	St Leonard's Church	Peter M Chalmers	1902-4	

Number	Name	Architect	Date	Commissioned by
Murray Park				
1		John Milne	1898	Charles Grubb
4		John Milne	c.1898	G. C. Douglas
6 & 8		David Henry	1897	
7-9		David Henry (att.)	c.1895	
10		David Henry	1897	W. Ramsay
11		Gillespie & Scott	1877	
12 & 14		David Henry	1901	Misses Murray
22		John Milne	1895	
23		John Milne	1895	
	Corner House, Murray Park & The Scores	John Milne	1896	G. C. Douglas
unlocated houses in Murray Pk		David Henry:		
		one	1894	Mr Swann
		three	1896	Mr Ramsay
		one	1898	Mr D. Bett
Murray Place				
3-5		David Henry	1896	Mr Ramsay
9-7		David Henry	1896	Mr David Bett
6, 8, 10	(2 houses and corner house)	David Henry	1898	Mr Ramsay
The Scores N = north S = south side				
S	Castlegate, East Scores	Hall & Henry	1879	David Henry
N	Castlecliffe	David Bryce	1869	Thomas Purdie
N	Edgecliffe	George Rae	1864-66	John MacGregor builder
S	Kennedy Hall	Gillespie & Scott	1895	
S	The Castle House			
N	Scores Park (now University House)	John Starforth	1864-66	Barton Graham of Morphie
N 11	Northcliffe	begun by Hall & Henry/ completed by Milne		Dr J Adamson

Number	Name	Architect	Date	Commissioned by
The Scores (cont)				
N north				
S south side				
N 15	Rockview		1864-66	Dr O Home Bell
S 10	The Swallowgate	R.R Anderson	1895	
S 12	Craigard	Jesse Hall	1863	D. McArthur
S 14-16	Clifton Bank (ltr StKatherine's Lodge)	Jesse Hall	1856	J. Paterson
S 18-20	cottages	David Henry	1895	W. Woodcock
N	The Presbytery	James Gillespie	1894	
N	St James Church	Reginald Fairlie	1910	
S	Canmore	Gillespie & Scott	1895	
S	The Russell Hotel	John Milne	1896	house for G.C. Douglas
S	Hazelbank Hotel	John Milne	1897	house for G.C. Douglas
S	New Halls (now Craigmount John Milne Nursing Home)		1897	house for G.W. Burnett
S 40-42	The St Andrews Golf Hotel	Hall & Henry (att.)	c.1895	
S 50	The Hirsel	David Henry (att.)	pre 1880	
S	Seaton House (Scores Hotel East)	George Rae	1864-5	J. Buddo
S	The Scores Hotel	John Milne	1880	
S	St Salvator's (Scores Hotel West)	John Milne (att.)	1880	
Gillespie Terrace				
No. 6		plan David Henry	1849-53	The Town Council
		reconstructed by Jesse Hall	1865	Rbt Chambers
3 & 4		George Rae		John B Melville
	The Grand Hotel	James Munro	1895	
	The R &A Clubhouse	George Rae	(opened: 1854)	

Number	Name	Architect	Date	Commissioned by
<u>**Queens Gardens**</u>				
corner South St	The Town Hall	J.A. Hamilton	1858-61	Town Council
2		David Rhind	1869	
3		William Scott (Dundee)	1857	
4		George Rae	1857	W. Stobie (to be general model for street)
5		George Rae (att.)	1860-63	
6 7 8 9 10 11		John Milne (att.)	1860	
12		John Milne (att.)	c.1859	
13/14		George Rae (att.)	1860-63	
15		John Milne	c.1859-60	
16		John Milne	1863	Thomas Rodger
17	(sculptured keystones)	Wm Walker, Leith		
18-21		John Milne (att.)	1859 on	
22				
23	St Regulus	George Rae	1865-65	J. McGregor
<u>**Queens Terrace**</u>				
	Annex to St Regulus	Gillespie & Scott	1893	
2 - 4		John Milne (att.)	1859 on	
15	Cowansrigg	David Henry (att.)	1879	G.W. Burnet
	The Episcopal Church Rectory	Gillespie & Scott	1869	
	St Andrews Episcopal Church	Sir R.R. Anderson	1867-69	

[(att.) = attributed to]

Appendix II

THE JUDICIAL REVIEW, 2000

In giving an outline from the Report on the Judicial Review, with each section I will state, briefly, Lord Bonomy's opinions and conclusions. These appear in italics to make it clear that they were not the comments he made in court. They are taken in order, except for the section which is headed 'Delay'. I will give Lord Bonomy's decision on that at the end of my account.

During the first day and a half Lord Mackay put forward the submission for the petitioners. They sought to have planning permission for Kingask quashed on the following grounds:

1. Fife Council erred in law by not requiring the developers to provide an environmental statement under the Environmental Assessment (Scotland) Regulations 1988.
2. The Council erred in law by failing to comply with their duties under the Town and Country Planning Act, Notification of Applications (Scotland) Direction 1997, by failing to consider whether the development involved a significant departure from the approved Structure Plan, thus requiring notification of the application to the Secretary of State/First Minister,* and by failing to notify him of the application as one involving a Site of Special Scientific Interest, in relation to which Scottish Natural Heritage have recommended conditions which the Council did not propose to attach to the planning permissions. The Purpose of notification is to enable the First Minister to consider whether he should take action with regard to the application.
3. The Council erred in law and exercised their discretion in an

unreasonable manner by granting the application without having due regard to the Development Plan in accordance with their duty under section 25 of the Town and Country Planning (Scotland) Act 1997.

4. The Council failed to give clear and intelligible reasons for their determination of the application, including whether or not it was in accordance with the development plan, and thus acted in a way which was unfair to the petitioners.

Lord Mackay presented the first two points as his principal broad heads, and the second two as bolstering these principal submissions. He spoke for the first day and a half.

The defence by Mr Reid, on behalf of the first respondents (Fife Council), and by Mr Martin on behalf of the developers took most of the next three days. On his third morning Mr Reid asked the Court to consider the preliminaries 'Title and Interest' and 'Mora (Delay)' first, and to pronounce on them. The Judge said he would rule on these later in the day. At lunchtime Lord Bonomy said that he would hear the whole case before giving a decision. This was one of the moments of hope for the petitioners. (But they had been advised not to build up hopes from instances when things seemed to go well.)

* I have shortened this to First Minister, the title after the Scottish Parliament was established.

Title and Interest

Mr Reid, supported by Mr Martin, made the submission that 'The petitioners lack title and interest to bring the proceedings'. However, the respondents dwelt only on the question of interest.

1. The Petitioners are not directly and prejudicially affected by the decision to grant planning permission. None of the petitioners

lived within the legal definition of 'Neighbours'. The petitioners resided between 2.5 km and over 5 km from the site.

2 Planning control was designed to regulate development in the public interest. The statutory scheme for the regulation of planning was not intended to confer new rights on members of the public to see that it was properly implemented. 'The petitioners are no different from any other members of the public' who might be affected by the traffic and, so on. Given such rights, 'any group of busybodies could contest Council decisions'. Another term used by Mr Martin in referring to the petitioners was 'sabre rattling'. (Perhaps they carried the sword of truth and justice!)

3. The objections of the petitioners had been heard by the Council. They had made no protest that the Council had not taken account of their representations.

Mr Martin dwelt on the failure of the petitioners to seek interim interdict or suspension of the development. This meant that by their own deliberate act they were contributing to the detrimental effects they were complaining about, because rapid progress was being made with the construction works. As a result, he submitted, their interest to bring the proceedings diminished by the day. That should be weighed against in determining whether they had sufficient interest to proceed.

> *Lord Bonomy rejected that submission since he considered that the question of interest has to be determined as at the date the petition is presented.*

Lord Mackay referred to the petitioners' claim that the first respondents acted illegally in granting the application by 'failing to require an environmental statement under the 1988 Regulations', that they were entitled to have their representations considered in the light of environmental information properly produced and consulted upon, and that did not happen.

> *(Judgment): The petitioners have an interest to challenge the grant because they aver that the representations which they made related to matters which they aver should have been dealt with and considered under materially different procedures as a matter of law. I am satisfied that the petitioners have a material interest in the real issue in the case such as an interest in law to bring these proceedings. The petitioners were perfectly entitled to bring these proceedings.*

Mora (Delay)

Mr Reid pointed out that the petition was raised nineteen weeks after the application was determined. His submission on this matter included these points:

1. In certain areas of administration of which planning was one, where administrative certainty was important, any delay which tended to undermine the good order of sound administration was sufficient on its own to bar challenge.
2. The delay involved in the knowledge that operations were being carried out by the developer ... led to an inference of acquiescence.
3. The delay, when taken with the prejudice that would undoubtedly be suffered by the Developers were the grant to be quashed, was such as to bar the proceedings. By the time the Petition was presented, work on the site in excess of £1.5 million had been completed. One month later the works amounted to well over £1 million more. The result of a successful petition would be to halt the development in its tracks pending further

consideration of the application – to the obvious prejudice of the second respondents and their employees. Were the application to be ultimately refused, an issue would arise over the partially built developments.

Lord Mackay submitted precedents where satisfactory reasons for a delay were considered acceptable. He described the programme of the petitioners (as given above). Fund raising had to take place. They took no action initially since the local Community Council were considering raising proceedings. He submitted that there was no basis for an inference of acquiescence, and there was not such delay and prejudice as to warrant refusing the petition. Any rule that could be given from English authority did not apply in Scotland. There is no Scottish authority in which a petition for a Judicial Review has been refused on grounds of delay alone in the absence of acquiesence or prejudice. Where orders or decisions are challenged by petition for a Judicial Review there is no statutory time limit.

Environmental statement

The regulations are set out under the Environmental Assessment (Scotland) Regulations 1988. Those implemented in Scotland are the United Kingdom's obligations to give effect to European Union Council Directive 85/337/EEC of 27 June 1985. In Lord Bonomy's report there are ten pages of extracts from these regulations. They deal with varying sets of circumstances. Mr Reid conceded that within four weeks of the receipt of an application for planning permission, the authority was bound to decide one way or another whether to require an environmental statement. He referred to various articles from the above Directive which in his opinion did or did not apply in the case of Kingask. He concluded that these articles did not require the second respondents to provide a statutory environmental statement. He said that the matter was considered and a view taken by experienced officials not to require an environmental statement. On questioning by Lord Bonomy, Mr Reid was not able to say whether the decision was made after one meeting or several meetings, by whom it was made, or when. On a further question from Lord Bonomy Mr Reid said that in the absence of any record he could not say when, by whom, or on what basis the decision was made. There was no record. Two documents were referred to by Mr Reid: one sets out that the Council's scheme of delegation authorised the officials to make the decision. The other sets out the factors which the planning authorities, through their officials, had to consult in arriving at the their decision.

> *Lord Bonomy refers to these as documents whose tendentious nature tended to indicate they were prepared for the purposes of this case. He did not consider they assisted since they may well have been written to deal with issues other than the question of whether a decision was taken during the relevant period.*

Mr Reid, later supported by Mr Martin, submitted that the existence of doubt about whether a decision was made was insufficient for the petitioners to succeed. It was for them to establish positively that the decision was not made. There was no onus on the planning authority to establish that it was.

Had the officials power to make the decision?

This point was debated at length, both sides giving references to precedents. Lord Mackay submitted that the matter was considered and a view taken by experienced officials *not* to require an environmental statement. He referred to a number of documents; he suggested that no decision had been made within the relevant period (i.e. within four weeks of the planning application). In relation to an earlier application for the same site, in January 1999, the East Area Development Committee had referred to 'an environmental statement being an exception in the case of a golf course development'; they also indicated that none had been required 'because more than enough environmental information had already been given'. These statements indicated the wrong test had been applied, and on that erroneous basis determination not to require one had been made prior to the application presently being considered. Lord Mackay referred to a statement given by Mr Martin that the Company had to rely on an agreement made with the planning authority that an environmental statement was not necessary, but that a landscape assessment and an ecological assessment should be made. Lord Mackay quoted precedents and submitted that the officials of the planning authority were not entitled to make the decision whether or not to require an environmental statement. Their decision should accordingly be quashed with the effect that the planning authority had failed to discharge its statutory duty.

Mr Reid's reply for the respondents rested on the long established and judicially recognised rule that power to act on behalf of an authority may be delegated by practice. He cited at length the case of the Dalziel School Board versus Scotch Education Department (1915) concerning the dismissal of a teacher, and heard by Lord Dundas whose decision on this case has remained unchallenged. Then he went on to analyse certain aspects of this case, and subsequently referred to others he considered relevant.

An extract from Lord Bonomy's report shows the complexity of the subject and of the debate.

> *Lord Bonomy agreed with Mr Reid that neither the importance of the particular decision to be made nor the identity of the decision making body as an organ of central government is the determining factor. The question is a mixed question of fact and law whether the power to make the decision was delegated to the officials who made it. It is plain on the authority of the Dalziel School Board that the power to make the decision about the information to be furnished to an*

authority in the course of their consideration of an application can be tacitly or impliedly delegated to officials by established practice. It is not necessary to classify the act or decision as 'procedural' before it is capable of such delegation. … The Council's own scheme of delegation must be read in the light of the opinions of the Dalziel School Board. In terms of that scheme the Head of Planning, and therefore officials acting under his authority, are authorised to determine all non-controversial planning applications. They accordingly have specific delegated authority to take all decisions along the way to such applications and that must include the decision whether or not to require an environmental statement. … In my opinion any practice of the planning authority whereby decisions, whether or not to require an environmental statement, are made by officials acting under the authority of the Head of Planning is entirely consistent with the scheme. There is no reason why delegation by established practice cannot exist with formal delegation. … The final question is whether the facts of the case bear out the contention that delegation was implied by established practice. In difficult cases, such as the present, a number of officials would discuss the question before making the decision. Mr Reid assured me that established practice has been followed in this case. As with the question whether the decision was made at all by officials, I find the information presented to me an unsatisfactory basis for determining the issue whether an established practice existed and was followed in the present case. … What has emerged is an argument not heralded in the headings based on which appears a rule about established practice which was not referred to in the document which appears to be the Council's own view of the effect of the scheme of delegation as sufficient in itself to delegate the necessary authority. This is further matter about which the Court would require further evidence.

On the assumption that a decision not to have an environmental statement was validly made, Lord Mackay submitted that the decision was one that no planning authority or official thereof with delegated power acting reasonably would have made. The material available prior to March 1999 included the following.

1. A landscape and visual Appraisal by Land Use Consultants (Tyldesley) was prepared on behalf of the developer in October 1998 with an addendum compiled in December 1998. Lord Mackay contended that it was impossible for any official who read these documents to say the proposed development would not be likely to have significant effects on the landscape. The October document concluded that there would be significant landscape and visual effects arising from major to minor. The addendum referring to the modifications in the design included '1.4. Construction and operation of the hotel and golf course will have significant effects on the landscape character of the site. These are likely to be adverse, but the landscape would mature in time. However the scale of the effect on the daytime view from St Andrews Walkway is initially judged to be of major significance and adverse to nature. After twenty five years the effect is predicted to be of no significance. ... The conclusion: overall however, based on the loss of existing agricultural landscape, the change in character is considered to be an adverse effect of major significance.'
2. Lord Mackay presented an affidavit of Mark Turnbull, a landscape architect with experience of landscape and environmental assessments. In it he expressed views on matters of law, such as the status of any guidance from the Secretary of State in interpreting the Regulations. Referring to Mr Tyldesley's report and the Appraisal and Addendum by Land Use Consultants, Mr Turnbull concluded that the expert advising the Council and the consultants advising the developer expressed clear views which

brought the application plainly within the scope of Regulation 6 as an annexe application where the proposed development would have significant effects on the environment by virtue of its nature, size or location.

3. A letter from the Scottish Natural Heritage dated 31 March 1999 objected to the development. Quoting: 'S.N.H. consider that the development will result in a total change to the existing landscape character and introduce a substantial amount of new development into the open coastal landscape. ... it will result in significant and adverse visual and landscape impacts. These impacts comprise loss of existing landscape character, adverse impact on the landscape setting of St Andrews, erosion of the landscape quality associated with the A.G.L.V. (Area of Great Landscape Value) and proximity of the development to the coast, and associated adverse impact on people's experience of the landscape and views from the coastal path.' Lord Mackay admitted that it was difficult to lay any weight on this objection since it was submitted after the expiry of the four week period, but he referred to previous letters from Scottish Natural Heritage (26 November 1998 and 15 January 1999) regarding the earlier applications for the site and said their view was plain.

In conclusion Lord Mackay submitted 'in all these circumstances the decision not to require an environmental statement flew on the face of reason and was unreasonable in the Wednesbury sense'.

Mr Reid began his reply by emphasising 'the high hurdle that had to be leapt to satisfy the test of irrationality. If an issue is debatable or there is room for differing views, then irrationality cannot be established.'

Mr Reid set out to demolish Lord Mackay's submission. The main points were:

1. In none of the documents which had been considered in Court and from none of the various bodies who had made objections, including The Preservation Trust (with the exception of the local Community Council), had it been suggested that an environmental assessment should be obtained. He also dwelt on the irrelevance of some documents because they did not come during the four weeks critical period for submission for an environmental assessment. The Land Use Consultants apparently did not consider one should be lodged. In any case they related to a spent application and were irrelevant to the present one.
2. Mr Turnbull's affidavit: Mr Reid submitted that Mr Turnbull recognised that it was a matter of judgement whether a development was likely to have significant environmental effects. He quoted from a report by Parr Partnership prepared for the developer in February 1999; the concluding view was: 'The development is situated almost two and a half miles from the nearest viewpoints in St Andrews, and with the landscaping measures proposed and the materials used, the hotel development in itself will barely be visible.'

In order to identify the threshold for the word 'significant' Mr Reid turned to guidelines issued by the Secretary of State from the S.D.D. circular no 13/1998 of July 1988. He discussed the three main types of projects given which would need an environmental assessment. In the case of Annex 3 'for projects with unusually complex and potentially adverse environmental effects … annex 3 indicated that fairly high thresholds were required before an E.A. would be required.' Mr Reid submitted that it is difficult to relate these to Kingask, as they generally concern developments involving nuisance and pollution rather than altered landscape and views. He submitted that 'significant' meant 'high' or 'major'.

In my opinion it is difficult to see that these references by Mr Reid make any real dent in the general thrust of the Land Use Consultant's Appraisal and Addendum which is plainly to the effect that the development was likely to result in significant effects on the environment. The real question is the context in which the word 'significant' was used in these reports. Mr Turnbull was the only one of the experts who expressed the view that an environmental statement ought to have been provided or required. However he went on to acknowledge that all issues likely to give rise to significant environmental effects were considered. What was particularly striking about Mr Turnbull's opinion was that, having subjected all the material before the Council to detailed scrutiny, he was unable to identify any relevant issue which had not been addressed. He pointed to omissions and deficiencies in the opinions expressed and advice given. However, he does not identify any environmental issue which was not brought to the attention of the planning authority and sufficiently identified in the course of the planning process to enable the public to make comment thereon. Against this background the question for the court to decide is whether there was room for the decision-maker to determine that the development was not likely to have a significant effect on the environment.

Lord Bonomy summed up by stating that two striking elements in Mr Reid's submission brought him to his decision:

1. The absence of such a suggestion from any source other than the Community Council, and in particular the absence of any suggestion from The St Andrews Preservation Trust, which made such a suggestion in

relation to another similar application (i.e. at Scooniehill).

2. The terms of the Scottish Office Guidance. In the light of these factors it could not be said that the decision-maker so deciding was acting irrationally.

Discretion

Mr Reid submitted that since the failure to require an environmental statement had no practical effect the Court ought to exercise discretion to refuse the petition. Lord Mackay maintained that the Court did not have such discretion in the face of a failure to comply with a specific obligation introduced into Regulations to give effect to a duty imposed by a European Directive.

Lord Bonomy refers to recent case in the Court of Appeal in London where the result was 'The Court must be satisfied that the objectives of the Directive are met. However, the Court retains a discretion, notwithstanding the absence of a statement ... to decline to quash a decision if the objectives are in substance achieved by the procedure followed ... including the provision of appropriate information in a comprehensible form, making the public aware of the environmental implications of a project, giving an opportunity to the public to express an opinion about it, and the decision-maker taking account of opinions expressed and making an overall assessment when reaching a conclusion. Lord Bonomy respectfully agreed with the statement by Lord Nimmo at the English Court of Appeal of the aims and objects of the Directive. There follows a consideration as to whether in this case the Council had followed these requirements.

Regarding the submission by Lord Mackay based on the affidavit by Mr Turnbull who claims that if an environmental assessment had been required there would have been two beneficial effects:

1. *A wider consultation and a longer consultation period. This might have resulted in responses which identified the deficiencies in the assessment of the impact of the development on the AGLV and the character of St Andrews and its landscape setting.*
2. *The environmental information would have been presented in a systematic form including a non-technical summary which would have enabled the findings of the studies and the mitigation methods to be more readily understood by non-experts and decision makers.*

> *The argument was that the additional publicity associated with the Environmental Assessment might have brought the issues to the attention of a wider public and brought more response. Lord Bonomy's Judgment was that what he regarded as most significant is that Mr Turnbull does not give any indication that either benefit would have resulted in any practical effect. The point he makes is that there is room for differing opinion.*

Mr Reid outlined the procedure the Council followed, the material actually presented to the Council, the opportunity given for further public comment on the material, the orderly presentation of the material and the careful consideration of all material available leading to the decision.

From the Judgment:

> *Lord Bonomy's opinion was that he was persuaded by Mr Reid's submission that nothing of substance was lost to the first respondents by failure to require an Environmental Statement; that the aims and objectives of both the Directive and the Regulations were achieved. Any breach was of form and not of substance.*
>
> *Lord Bonomy outlines the aims and four other objectives of the Directive and Regulations.*

1. The provision of appropriate information in comprehensible form. There was no complaint from the petitioners.

2. Making the public aware of the environmental implications: it is abundantly plain that the public were aware of the potential environmental implications.

3. Giving the public an opportunity to express opinions about a development. The report refers to the meeting of 17 June where opinions were expressed.

4. The decision-maker should take into account the opinions expressed and make an overall assessment when reaching a conclusion. When the decision to grant the application was made at the meeting of the Strategic Development Committee it was by 12 votes to 5 against an amendment that the application should be turned down on the grounds that the development would by virtue of its size and location detrimentally affect an area of great landscape value and adversely impact on views on the coastal footpath, that the development would adversely affect landscape immunity, reduce the quality of the environment and the landscape setting of St Andrews, and that the development would create unacceptable traffic congestion in and around St Andrews, reduce road safety and affect adversely residential amenity.

> *Lord Bonomy was of the opinion that the decision was made in light of a consideration of all relevant environmental issues, and that the requirement upon the developer to provide an environmental statement would not have resulted in additional material of any significance being made available to the first respondents. It follows that nothing would have been gained by quashing the decision made and requiring the reprocessing and reconsideration of the application in the light of an environmental statement.*

Failure to notify the First Minister

Lord Mackay claimed that the application had to be notified because it involved a development which was a significant departure from the development plan. The relevant terms from the schedule were quoted.

> As a site of special scientific interest: the Scottish Natural Heritage had informed the Council that the proposed development would adversely affect such a site and advised against granting planning permission. He presented a 'variation of the case' in that Scottish Natural Heritage had recommended conditions to be attached to the planning permission.
>
> *Lord Bonomy: Scotish Natural Heritage did not indicate that development would adversely affect the site; in my opinion paragraph 10 did not apply. In the SNH's letter of 31 March there is a reference to what SNH 'hope may happen' and their 'wish to be consulted'. At the Hearing in June they again expressed their 'wish' to be consulted.*

The question of departure from the development plan

Lord Mackay argued this must mean the Structure Plan as the Local Plan had not then been approved by the First Minister. In regard to policy ED13 which states 'There is a presumption against development which would permanently remove or reduce the quality of prime agricultural land.'

Mr Reid: No question arose of a reduction in the quality of prime agricultural land. The question was one of the permanent removal thereof. The permanent removal only arose in relation to the built part of the development. It was advised that it is the policy of the Scottish Office of Agriculture and Fisheries Department where the built part of the development involved less than 10 hectares, as this one did, it is unobjectionable.

Lord Mackay maintained that was irrelevant since the policy related to the permanent removal of any prime agricultural land.

> *Lord Bonomy's judgment stated that he did not agree that this policy can only be read that way. '…it does not seem to me that it would necessarily be a significant departure from that policy to approve a development which includes an element of permanent removal of agricultural land within the range which the Department regard as acceptable. The problem with the Council's position is that the briefing papers for the various meetings make no reference to the 10 hectares guidance.'*

Lord Mackay: The strategy of the Structure Plan does not support development within areas of Great Landscape Value which will have a detrimental effect on the landscape. …

> *Whether a development will have a detrimental effect on the landscape is a matter of judgement and opinion.*

Lord Mackay: The commentary indicated that exceptions may only be allowed where the developer can demonstrate an over-riding need for the development on national or regional grounds which cannot be accommodated elsewhere. He submitted that there was no evidence that this was so in the case of Kingask; that there was no evidence in the documents regarding the question of an overriding need, nor that they had considered the absence of any other place where it might have been accommodated. Mr Reid, supported by Mr Martin, contested this, referring to occasions when this had been considered. He submitted that in the end it was a matter for the judgement of the planning authority. The final advice given by the Head of Planning before the decisive meeting was: 'Support for this document does not require the abandonment of planning policies. I recommend planning consent should be given subject to planning considerations under Section 75 Agreement'. The Council's statement to the meeting was 'The Council is satisfied that the proposed development is acceptable, subject to approved planning conditions and delivery of the Section 75 Agreement, the conditions of which have already been approved by the Council'.

> *Lord Bonomy: What is not at all clear is what the Council actually decided in relation to the Development Plan. Did they decide that the application did not involve a significant departure? Alternatively if they decided that it did, was the departure justified on planning grounds? In the latter case, of course, they were bound to notify the SOS/First Minister.*

Judgment

> *It is not clear from the statement what the First Respondents decided in relation to the question of development on prime agricultural land, or the impact of the development on the Area of Great Landscape Value. The statement as it stands does not tell me what the Council decided in relation to departure from the Development Plan. The reasons given are not clear. The Council have not given adequate reason for granting the application in respect that they have not stated clearly what their position was in relation to the Development Plan. Had it been necessary Lord Bonomy would have appointed a Second Hearing to clarify the points on which he had expressed doubt.*

Now we come to the conclusion reached. The matter in law which decided the case was that of Delay.

> *There was no material presented to me that the petitioners gave notice to the respondents that they intended to challenge the*

grant. When the campaign to raise funds went public on 18 October the second respondents became aware of it and were quoted a few days later in the local paper in terms designed to discourage support.

If the petition had been determined … in favour of the petitioners the disruptive consequences would have been such as to give a clear picture of a system lacking in proper control over planning.

In my opinion the fundraising which was not apparently embarked on until 18 October, and the obtaining of legal advice which was spread over a considerable period of time in which no significant additional information came to light do not satisfactorily explain the lapse of time before the proceedings were brought, particularly the period between the beginning of August and 17 November. I do not consider that the petition was presented promptly. Between 3 August and 18 October there was no public indication given of an impending challenge. Thereafter a further month elapsed before the petition was presented. Meanwhile substantial works were being undertaken on the site to the knowledge of the petitioners. … The success of any petition presented so long after the event as this one is bound to have a significant adverse effect on the good administration of planning control in the St Andrews area which must have been obvious to the petitioners.

For these reasons I consider that the delay in bringing the proceedings is such that when it is combined with the petitioners' apparent acquiescence in the grant, the disruptive effect of a late challenge would have in good administration if successful and the prejudice to the second respondents of bringing the proceedings so late, that this is a case in which it is appropriate to sustain the plea of mora and dismiss the petition.

At a later hearing regarding expenses, Lord Bonomy said that he had decided to depart from the usual rule of 'Expenses followed success'. He was unhappy about the role of the Local Authority in certain matters and would require the Petitioners to pay only 50% of the costs. This meant these costs could be met through the amount raised from fund-raising.

BIBLIOGRAPHY

Bruce, George — *Reminiscences and Wrecks of St Andrews Bay.* Dundee: Leng & Co., 1884

Campbell, Alex — *St Andrews Directory, a Classified List of Trades and Professions in Fife 1820-1870,* 2 vols., 1894 (typed). Kirkcaldy

Cant, R.G. — *The University of St Andrews. A Short History.* Oliver & Boyd, 1946, revised 1992

Clark, Alwyn — *The McKenzie Sisters.* Black Ace Books, 1996

Cook, Helen — *Old St Andrews.* Catrine: Stenlake Publishing, 2001

Fordyce, T.T. — *Memoirs of a Provost 1896-1980.* St Andrews: Alvie Publication, 1981

Freud, Sigmund — *The Interpretation of Dreams.* Standard Edition of *The Complete Psychology of Sigmund Freud Vols 4 & 5.* London: Hogarth Press and The Institute of Psychology, 1962

Frew, John (editor) — *Building for a New Age: The Architects of Victorian and Edwardian St Andrews.* St Andrews: Crawford Centre, 1984

Gifford, John — *The Buildings of Scotland: Fife.* Penguin Pevsner Series, 1988

Grimond, Jo	*The St Andrews of Jo Grimond.* Allan Sutton, 1992
Hall, Ursula	*St Andrew and Scotland.* The University of St Andrews Library, 1994
Irvine, Mabel	*The Avenue of Years. A Memoir of Sir James Irvine.* Edinburgh: Blackwood, 1970
Kirk, Russell	*St Andrews.* London: B.T. Batsford, 1954
Lamont Brown, Ray	*Scotland in Old Photographs.* St Andrews: Alan Sutton, 1996
Lyle, David	*Shadow of St Andrews Past.* John Donald, 1989
Lyle, David	*Images of St Andrews Past.* St Andrews: St Nicholas Press, 1994
McDougall, William	*Social Psychology.* London, 1928
Reid, Alistair	*Weathering.* Edinburgh: Canongate, 1978
St Andrews Preservation Trust	*Annual Reports and Year Books 1938-2000*
St Andrews Preservation Trust	*Conservation in St Andrews. A Survey of the Work of the Preservation Trust,* 1963, revised 1968, 1975, 1989

St Andrews Preservation Trust — *Trees in St Andrews*, by J.A. Macdonald, 2nd edn, 1977

St Andrews Preservation Trust — *Three Decades of Historical Notes*, edited by Mary Innes and Joan Whelan, 1991

St Andrews Preservation Trust — *A Journey through the Lade Braes*, by Matthew Jarron & Jennifer Webster, 2000

Stout, F.G. — *Manual of Psychology*. London 1898

Wilson, George — *Official St Andrews Directory 1894, 1898, 1907, 1909, 1913, 1926, 1932, 1935, 1939, 1940*. St Andrews Times

Cover Design
and Layout: Stephen M.L. Young
Elgin
Scotland
stephenmlyoung@aol.com

Font: Adobe Garamond (11pt)

Copies of this book can be ordered via the Internet:

www.librario.com

or from:

Librario Publishing Ltd
Brough House
Milton Brodie
Kinloss
Moray IV36 2UA
Tel /Fax No 01343 850 617